Onward Alone

Caroline Prohosky

Covenant Communications, Inc.

Cover images: main image reference photo by McKenzie Deakins. For more information visit http://www. photographybymckenzie.com Background Image:*Facing the Frontier* © Glen S. Hopkinson. For more information, go to www.glenhopkinson.com.

Cover design copyright © 2013 by Covenant Communications, Inc.

Published by Covenant Communications, Inc.
American Fork, Utah

Printed in the United States of America
First Printing: March 2013

19 18 17 16 15 14 13   10 9 8 7 6 5 4 3 2 1

ISBN 978-1-62108-070-1

Dedication

This book is dedicated to
my sister Cathy,
who has stood by me
with love and wisdom
every single moment
of my life

and

To all of my sisters.

I have said little about the Mormon women. I have scarcely alluded to them, because my memories of them are [of such reverence] that I cannot think of their character as a theme for discussion. In one word, it was eminently that which for Americans dignifies the names of mother, wife, and sister. Of the self-denying generosity which went to ennoble the whole people in my eyes, I witnessed among them the brightest illustrations. I have seen the ideal Charity of the statue gallery surpassed by the young Mormon mother, who shared with the stranger's orphan the breast of milk of her own child.

—Colonel Thomas L. Kane (Howe, 420)

Acknowledgments

DEEPEST GRATITUDE AND APPRECIATION TO:

R. Don Oscarson, whose idea it was to create a film based on the lives of these elect women and whose vision and energy sustained me through the duration of this project.

Russ Richins, who has been not only an excellent producer of the film and the liaison for the book but who has also stood by me as a close friend and artistic associate.

Shirley Maynes, whose lifelong research provided the basis for this project. I have relied on her research, and much of her personal expression and individual charm has found its way into this book. She was a dear friend whose sincere love for the Mormon Battalion pioneer women permeated her life.

Kathryn Jenkins Gordon, whose faith and expertise were invaluable and whose professionalism and friendship were inspiring.

Aaron Shaw, who meticulously analyzed the first draft, contributing vision and encouragement through the completion of the book.

Roxanne Grey, who wrote expressive prose for Elizabeth Harris Browett, Clarissa and Louisa Canfield, Alice Clayton Martin, and Margaret Jane Willis.

Teresa Hishop, whose final editing enriched clarity and poetic expression of the book as it was brought to fruition. I am grateful for her collaboration on the chapter headings.

Allison Zobell, for invaluable foundational research and writing.

Those involved with the film: I am deeply indebted to those who contributed financially to the making of the film. I am grateful to Lee Wakefield, who believed in this project and helped with the financial planning for the film. I am grateful to Jake and Michelle Black for initial research. I feel a deep sense of gratitude to Tom Lefler, Jacob Moffat, Jon Anderson, and Emmy Paiser, who helped me during the production process of the film. I am especially appreciative to the faculty of the Department of Dance at Brigham Young University, who sustained me through the long duration of this endeavor and many of whom contributed time and artistry to the development and realization the film.

The nature of sacrifice teaches that faith is not trying to believe regardless of evidence; rather, it is daring to act regardless of consequences. These women dared. They acted. They sacrificed.

Introduction

THE INFLUENCE OF HISTORY IS a perpetual living force. Our current thoughts and hopes, our immediate expectations and fears are shaped by history. The greater our understanding of the past, the more capability we have to reidentify and alter our present. History is our supportive friend and ally.

As we connect with people from the past and participate in their experiences, we are instinctively educated. I believe that when we learn about courageous and righteous people, we can be intuitively refined and uplifted.

The early pioneers of The Church of Jesus Christ of Latter-day Saints were courageous and righteous people who built a gospel framework that will support and uphold truth into and through the last dispensation. Separated from the materiality of the world through persecution and loss of property—and sometimes through loss of family and community—they built their own communities unlike any before. They are a people of history who we should understand and with whom we should unite.

Moreover, I personally believe that the Mormon Battalion is a central defining moment in the building of strength and solidarity that would come to exist in The Church of Jesus Christ of Latter-day Saints. The people involved in this event responded to one of the most faith-challenging requests in Church history.

This moment was a superlative test of devotion for the Saints in various respects.

First, how would the early members respond to Brigham Young as a prophet when he issued such a seemingly impossible request? The Saints had followed him onto uncivilized and uncultivated prairie lands under the harshest of conditions—would they now honor his request to send men away from wives and children, most of whom were living in the most dire of circumstances? Was Brigham Young really called of God? The Saints responded in a way that confirmed their trust in the procedural order of the Lord: the mantle had been passed from one prophet to another. Obviously, this acceptance of Church procedure was absolutely imperative for the continuance and growth of the Church. In affirmation, on the stark and forsaken prairie in 1846, Brigham Young was accepted as the mouthpiece of the Lord on the deepest possible level.

Second, this was a moment in which the Saints needed to decide what they thought about America as their mother country. Were they still loyal Americans? And would they support a government that had woefully failed to protect them? They would, and they did. Third, and of greatest magnitude, did the Saints truly trust in their God? Women and children would be left as refugees, alone on an untamed and unknown land with little or no provision or shelter. Would Heavenly Father take care of them? Would Heavenly Father also care for and protect the men who would undertake the longest military march in history—more than two thousand miles, all of it through uncharted and unfriendly territory, to fight an uncertain war? Would these soldiers of faith survive? Most of them did. So did most of their wives.

And finally, dire living conditions would test the capacity of charity among the Saints. It would have been impossible for these early members to survive this sacrifice without dedication of all personal talents and abilities to the welfare of the entire community. Charity prevailed, and the people not only survived but, in many instances, flourished.

For me, the event of the Mormon Battalion is a quintessential moment in which The Church of Jesus Christ of Latter-day Saints was tested, defined, and firmly established in the hearts of the people who began to build Zion. The Mormon Battalion chapter of history marked, in its own way, a new beginning and understanding of the far reach of faith and its power to shape our lives.

The women who remained on the prairie, watching their husbands march away, were a magnificent part of that faith-testing moment of history. Their stories are astounding. It has been a joy to examine the histories of this specific sector of pioneer women who helped build a new construct of religious life. The wives, mothers, and sisters of the men who marched in the Mormon Battalion have their own stories to share.

The perils of the Mormon Battalion soldiers were many and severe, and a reasonable amount of documentation of the actual march and related events gives us great insight into the hazardous journey. However, little has been said of the families who waited on the plains of Iowa and Nebraska. In the pages of this book, I hope to tell some of the equally compelling stories of the women who remained behind on the untamed prairie.

In presenting these women, there are five informational points that I wish to share.

First, I have treasured and relied on the research of Shirley Maynes. I did not examine all of the primary documents that she investigated, but rather sifted and distilled some of the content of her work, adding some authentic pioneer writings where possible. From her book, I extracted names, dates, and essential events of these women's lives. I have not footnoted each particular date or event in the lives of the individual women; rather, I refer readers to her work, *Five Hundred Wagons Stood Still*, for further information and documentation.

Second, I have corrected some of the punctuation and spelling of the original pioneer documents to improve ease and flow, eliminate distraction, and enable readers to more readily grasp the essence of the quoted material. I have documented the sources of each of the authentic writings included in this book so that readers may refer to those writings if desired.

Third, while the early Saints enjoyed great friendships with many Native American people, especially through the trying days of Winter Quarters, there were also instances when the pioneers feared certain tribes. Their apprehensions are sometimes reflected in their writings. I have not altered the writings, but rather ask readers to understand the time and historical context from which these writings emerged and to read with care and discretion, not taking offense in any way. Certainly no offense was intended.

Fourth, as the ten to fifteen thousand refugees arrived on the plains in 1846, they covered a vast area of land that included both Iowa and

Nebraska. Rather than naming both Iowa and Nebraska when referring to the plains where the refugees temporarily settled, I have simply referred to the area as "Iowa."

Finally, I wish to clarify that there were some women who traveled with the battalion as laundresses. The biographies of those women provide another collection of inspiring and fascinating narratives. However, the stories in this book are limited to those women who remained on the plains when the battalion marched away.

This book does not provide an in-depth account of each woman's life history. Rather, I have presented a brief biography emphasizing the distinctive events that individualized each woman. Where appropriate, the basic biographies are accompanied and enriched by thoughts, ideas, and poetry that accentuate the theme of each woman's life.

May the spirits of these women delight and enlighten, comfort, and strengthen your hearts as they have mine.

—Caroline Jean Prohosky

THE EXODUS

BREWING IN THE ONCE-PEACEFUL CITY of Nauvoo was a boisterous and ill-tempered storm, thundering with threats and accusations, rumbling with reckless gunfire and blazing farmlands. Inflamed conflicts endangered members of the early Mormon Church from every direction. In 1845, the tempest temporarily quieted when the Saints acquiesced to the demands of the Quincy Committee, a council of seven people who endeavored to negotiate peace between Mormons and neighboring residents. The committee insisted on a full and unconditional surrender of Church members, who hesitantly and somberly agreed to leave the following May, as soon as property could be sold and weather conditions permitted.

Neighboring residents, however, were not patient. They would not wait until May. Empowered by inaction of the federal and state governments, the citizenry demanded a complete and immediate midwinter evacuation. The Saints were forced to relinquish the keys to their beloved temple, abandon their homes, and flee across the Mississippi River. Mob brutality had prevailed (see Maynes, 1).

As early as February 1844, Church leaders had begun discussing the idea of moving the entire Church west. Joseph Smith had originally conceptualized the western migration, and after his death the new Church leaders began earnest preparations (see Kelly, 279). As the exodus grew undeniably imminent, the Saints worked with great urgency and determination to complete the Nauvoo Temple. As President Brigham Young declared, "We want to build the Temple in this place, [even] if we have to do it as the Jews built the walls of the temple in Jerusalem, with a sword in one hand and the trowel in the other" (Kelly, 278).

In October 1845, ordinance work began in the partially completed temple. As winter approached, the Saints worked with ever-increasing resolve to receive the blessings of the temple before their inevitable departure from the city. Many members of the Church had already left Nauvoo by the time their sacred building was completed and dedicated on April 30, 1846 (see Maynes, 1). As early as February 1846, more than two months before completion and dedication of the temple, Church members began fleeing Nauvoo by way of the frozen Mississippi River. With below-zero winds biting through clothing and penetrating the thin canvas of covered wagons, the Saints departed into a wintry unknown.

The exodus continued through the following year. Mason Brayman, an attorney who helped arrange an agreement whereby members of the Church could leave Illinois, described the mass evacuations:

> This scene of confusion, fright and distress was continued throughout the forenoon. In every part of the city scenes of destitution, misery and woe met the eye. Families were hurrying away from their homes, without a shelter,—without means of conveyance,—without tents, money, or a day's provision, with as much of their household stuff as they could carry in their hands. Sick men and women were carried upon their beds—weary mothers, with helpless babes dying in the arms, hurried away—all fleeing, they scarcely knew or cared whither, so it was from their enemies, whom they feared more than the waves of the Mississippi, or the heat, and hunger and lingering life and dreaded death of the prairies on which they were about to be cast. The ferry boats were crowded, and the river bank was lined with anxious fugitives, sadly awaiting their turn to pass over and take up their solitary march to the wilderness. (Linn, Chapter 20, "Illinois—The Evacuation of Nauvoo")

Exile from home and community was not new to the Saints, and this was not the first time they had left a temple behind them. However, giving up Nauvoo was perhaps the most difficult surrender for the members of the young Church. The new temple had been a symbol of hope and permanence. Its glistening walls had also been a symbol of the promise that God's presence would be with the Saints at all times. Though they may not have realized it at the time, the refugees would come to rely more fervently on this promise with every step they took into an intimidating wilderness.

After the February crossing on the Mississippi ice, the Saints continued their evacuation through the spring and into the summer. Men, women, and children traveled from Nauvoo to Sugar Creek, on to Garden Grove, then onward to Mount Pisgah before finally arriving in Council Bluffs and Winter Quarters on the border of Iowa and Nebraska, a total distance of about three hundred miles.

Eventually there was relief from the cold, but the spring season introduced a different assortment of difficulties. Constant rains and melting snows created deep, heavy, muddy quagmires across the entire state of Iowa. Brigham Young Jr. described the slow and ponderous journey of the Saints who were weighed down in the mire:

> Traveling through the swamps and bogs of Iowa was slow and painful in the extreme. For miles and miles the wagons labored heavily over corduroy road, or rather a bridge made of logs lashed together with tough willows. The terrible swamp was full of danger and difficulty. Here and there were swells or moors with a little sod over seas of water and mud below. If one wagon got across a swell in safety no other would dare follow in its tracks, for they would have sunk out of sight. Each wagon straddled the tracks of the last, and even then the wheels would sink through the twelve-inch sod into the muddy lake below, and sometimes hours would be consumed in traversing a quarter of a mile. (Kelly, 282)

Mary Ann Stearns, one of the women driven out of Nauvoo, recalled, "The anguish and suspense of those dreadful hours can never be told in words." Then she added, "I will never forget the unflinching force and courage of the devoted group of women. They never thought of fleeing or turning away" (Maynes, 2).

The prophet Brigham Young, who had been the leader of the Church for a mere eighteen months, said of this daunting moment:

> I did not think there had ever been a body of people since the days of Enoch, placed under the same unpleasant circumstances that the people have been where there was so very little grumbling, and I was satisfied that the Lord was pleased with the majority of the Camp of Israel. (Maynes, 3)

Many Saints did not reach their prairie destination of Council Bluffs or Winter Quarters, or one of the nearby areas, until July. As they began to construct temporary prairie settlements, five hundred men were called to march away from the refugee camp to fight a war—leaving wives, mothers, sisters, daughters, and sons to the mercy of the elements of nature and the kindness of neighbors. They put all their faith, hope, and trust in the Lord as their protectorate, guide, and comforter. And then they marched away.

BATTALION BEGINNINGS:

The Call to Arms

Battalion soldier Sergeant Daniel Tyler provided a well-defined account of the thoughts and feelings that existed in the camp when the battalion call sounded in 1881 when he penned *A Concise History of the Mormon Battalion in the Mexican War*, exposing the deepest sentiments that ran through the minds of the Saints as they contemplated their situation:

> Kind reader, if you can fancy yourself banished from civilization, ostracized, your Government failing to redress your wrongs; your best friends and leading citizens murdered in cold blood, when held as prisoners, under the plighted faith of your State for their protection; yourselves and families fleeing before ruthless mobs during one of the coldest winters ever known in the Western States; many sick, and all short of provisions, living to a considerable extent on short rations of parched corn or corn meal.
>
> Imagine that no luxuries or palatable food for the sick were to be had except a quantity of quails sent by Divine Providence into your camp, nay more, into your tents and seeking to conceal themselves under the very bedding where your sick wife or child or even your aged father lay (and him perhaps a revolutionary soldier who had fought many a hard battle to gain his and your liberty,) and perhaps under the couch of that mother who had given you life and cared for your tender years, whose emaciated face and sinking and tottering limbs you had fondly hoped to make happy and comfortable in her declining years.

Then picture your beloved wife and little ones, not now in the cold February storms, but in an almost tropical July sun, without house or home, perhaps living in a tent and perhaps only a mere wagon with one yoke of oxen, and in Indian country.

Fancy the penalty of returning to civilization to be death. . . .

Then suppose you had petitioned every officer, from the justice of the peace to the chief executive of the nation to redress your wrongs, and that the only satisfaction given was, "Your cause is just, but I can do nothing for you."

Suppose your patriotism had induced you to leave—not home, being without a home to leave—but your family, in an Indian country, without food, and, at the call of your country, had enlisted to aid in the suppression of the common enemy, and served for months without news from your family. . . .

If you can imagine all of these facts are your own experience, you may have a faint idea of the feelings and emotions of this loyal band of solders. (Tyler, 198–199)

In the summer of 1846, a desperate Brigham Young had sent a messenger to Washington, DC, with a plea for help and protection. President Young offered the services of the Church to haul provisions for the army, to establish posts, or to render any service needed in order to earn money to buy supplies, wagons, and teams for the westward trek.

These proposals were not accepted. It would be interesting to look back into history and observe President Young's reaction when the messenger returned bearing a demand for five hundred of the most able-bodied men to march to California as soldiers to fight in the Mexican-American War (see Ricketts, 2). Instead of offering desperately needed protection for the Saints, the government was asking for wartime assistance.

It is likely that Brigham Young felt himself in a quandary. He knew that the Mormon men had no desire to be soldiers. He knew these men had given every last strain of nerve and sinew to protect their families, often at the peril of their lives. Now he would ask these same men to leave wives and children, most of whom were huddled in wagon boxes and dugouts, and undertake what would become the longest infantry march in history—walking from Winter Quarters, Nebraska, to Fort Leavenworth, Kansas, and then on to San Diego, California.

Nonetheless, President Brigham Young's faith in his Heavenly Father and his confidence in the Saints triumphed as his voice echoed through the camp:

> You are now going into an enemy's land at your country's call. If you live your religion and respect your officers, and hold sacred the property of the people among whom you travel, and never take anything but what you pay for; I promise you in the name of Israel's God that not one of you shall fall by the hand of the enemy. Though there will be battles fought in your front and in your rear, on your right hand and on your left, you will not have any fighting to do except with wild beasts. (Ricketts, 6)

The irony of the government's request did not escape many of those who were asked to march in the battalion. Zadock K. Judd, for one, found it contradictory to be asked to fight for a country that was built on a pledge of religious freedom but that had permitted innocent people to be persecuted because of personal religious beliefs. Despite perceptions of flagrant injustices on the part of the government, Judd found within himself a deep reserve of faith perhaps not previously recognized. He wrote:

> It was quite a hard pill to swallow—to leave wives and children on the wild prairies, destitute and almost helpless, having nothing to rely on only the kindness of neighbors, and go to fight the battles of a government that had allowed some of its citizens to drive us from our homes, but the word comes from the right source and seemed to bring the spirit of conviction of its truth with it and there was quite a number of our company volunteered, myself and brother among them. (Ricketts, 6)

Zadock Judd was not alone in his faith in President Brigham Young. The early Saints who were clustered together at Council Bluffs and Winter

Quarters trusted their prophet and heeded his "call to arms." Over a period of three weeks, five companies, each consisting of one hundred men, were assembled (Tyler, 113–118).

The Night Before

BEFORE THE MORMON BATTALION MARCHED away, President Young insisted there be a dance for all the people in the camp. Preparations commenced. Men who would soon be marching off to war cleared a wide space and stamped the grass down until it was smooth enough for dancing. The members of Captain Pitt's Brass Band tuned their instruments. The air was filled with music, dance, and merriment until the sun skirted the western horizon. As the festivities came to a close, a pleased Brigham Young exclaimed, "Well, I declare, this beats all the parties I have ever seen here" (Tyler, 351).

Colonel Thomas L. Kane took particular note of the women who had gathered for one last celebration before bidding their husbands good-bye:

> There was no sentimental affection at their leave-taking. The afternoon before was appropriated to a farewell ball; and a more merry dancing rout I have never seen, though the company went without refreshments, and their ball-room was of the most primitive.
>
> If anything told the Mormons had been bred to other lives, it was the appearance of the women, as they assembled here. Before their flight they had sold their watches and trinkets as the most available resource for raising ready money; and hence, like their partners, who wore waistcoats cut with useless watch-pockets, they, although their ears were pierced and bore the loop-marks of rejected pendants, appeared without ear-rings, chains or brooches. Except [for the absence of] such ornaments, however, they lacked nothing, most becoming the attire of decorous maidens. (Howe, 424)

The refugees celebrated with zeal. Colonel Kane continued:

> With the rest, attended the elders of the church within call, including nearly all the chiefs of the High Council, with their wives and children. They, the gravest and most trouble-worn, seemed the most anxious of any to be first to throw off the burden of heavy thoughts. Their leading of the dancing in a great double cotillion was the signal for the festivity to commence.
>
> Light hearts, lithe figures, and light feet, had it their own way from an early hour until after the sun had dipped behind the sharp sky line of the Omaha hills. Silence was then called, and a well cultivated mezzo soprano voice belonging to a young lady with fair face and dark eyes, gave with quartette accompaniment a little song,—a version of the text, touching to all earthy wanderers:
> "By the rivers of Babylon we sat down and wept.
> *"We wept when we remembered Zion."*
> There was danger of some expression of feeling when the song was over, for it had begun to draw tears; but breaking the quiet with his hard voice, an elder asked the blessing of Heaven on all . . . and then, all dispersed, hastening to cover from the falling dews. (Howe, 424)

On July 20, 1846, the men marched away.

* * *

"If thou art merry, praise the Lord with singing, with music, with dancing, and with a prayer of praise and thanksgiving." —D&C 136:28

Revelation received by President Brigham Young at Winter Quarters, January 1847

Leave-Takings

ALTHOUGH THE SAINTS SAW THE vision and felt the spirit of the rightness of the battalion call, the farewells on the morning of departure reverberated with tones of abandonment, desertion, and desolation. Mary Bettice Compton was left with only the frayed canvas cover an of old wagon stretched along a fence as protection for her and her five children; one might imagine her standing mutely at its edge, watching as her husband walked away (see Maynes, 137). William Wallace Casper left his young wife, Sarah Ann Bean Casper, crying in the street with her nine-month-old daughter, Sarah Jane, cradled in her arms (see Maynes, 108).

"I enlisted and left that very day for Council Bluffs," wrote Newman Bulkley as he left his loved ones in tears. His wife, Jane, and son, Nephi, were camped in a solitary wagon at the side of the road with barely enough provisions to last a month.

Worry and anxiety encompassed other Saints as well. Edward Hunter left his wife, Mary Ann, and his two-year-old daughter "on the prairie without a home or income to the care of their Heavenly Father and the Saints" (Maynes, 284). Zacheus Cheney perhaps expressed it best when he wrote of that morning: "I tell you that on that day, the tears fell like rain drops" (Ricketts, 17).

PRAIRIE RAIN

Tears.
Some were quiet
And indiscreet.

Other tears
were accompanied by sobs
That pounded heavily,
Lacerating each breath
With the grasping and clutching of
Inner deluge.

Tears
Dampened the prairie ground
And sank down into the soil
of Iowa and Nebraska.

Tears
Overwatered the eyes
That were cast upward,
Searching the heights of the sky,

Tears
Traced small tributaries
On the faces that were
Marching westward
Toward Fort Leavenworth.

Tears
Poured from hearts
And hopes.

But always,
The quiet and gentle
Unfolding of the Spirit
Reminds us.

Tears
Have power to cleanse our vision
And baptize our hearts.

                         —C. Prohosky

Left Behind

MOST OF THE WOMEN LEFT behind were young—between the ages of eighteen and thirty-five. One of the youngest wives, Elizabeth Ann Meyers Glines joined the Church at age thirteen, married at fourteen, and watched her husband march away with the battalion when she was only fifteen. At the older end of the spectrum, Sarah Elizabeth Reynolds Haskell joined the Church at age forty-two and was fifty when she bid her husband farewell. Elizabeth and David Pettegrew were both fifty-four years old the day David marched away with the battalion.

The women who remained on the plains were from diverse circumstances. Most of the wives, sisters, and mothers were from the United States, but others had traveled impressive distances, immigrating from countries such as England, Canada, Scotland, Ireland, Wales, Sweden, and Germany. Some of the women who sent men into the battalion had not even been baptized members of the Church. One woman, fifty-eight-year-old Polly Pierce Knight Elmer, was not baptized until four years later in the Salt Lake Valley in 1850 (see Maynes, 182).

Not all of the women whose husbands joined the battalion stayed in Iowa. At least eight women are known to have returned to their homes in the East, and a number of those marriages continued through transcontinental letters for years—some for a lifetime.

But most of the women remained at Council Bluffs and Winter Quarters, supporting their husbands in accepting the call to arms. In fact, displaying uncommon courage, a number of women sent more than one family member away in the battalion. Lucretia Haws Sessions sent not only her husband but also two sons and a daughter-in-law marching across the continent with the battalion (see Maynes, 410).

The women who waved good-bye to their husbands, sons, and brothers may not have marched with the battalion but, in a sense, they were not "left behind." Temporally these women may have remained on the windswept plains of Iowa, but spiritually they moved forward and onward. They may have *felt* alone, but they moved onward precisely because they were *not* alone. In their unforeseen extremities, they came to know their Savior in ways they never had before. With His guidance, these women faced enormous difficulties, and in doing so, they saw the world anew. They looked at life through new filters of compassion, fearlessness, and patience, and saw new magnitudes of dignity, heroism, and hope. Their Savior's name had come to be written in their hearts. And with uncharacteristic faith and valor, they gathered their children and moved onward.

THE WOMEN:

Loss

Loss was a given for the early Saints. Some were disinherited when they joined the Church, losing precious family ties. Loss of friendships persisted as new converts were rejected by their communities. The loss of property became commonplace as persecution forced the Saints to abandon one home after another across the wide expanse of Ohio, Missouri, and Illinois. The entire Church experienced a devastating and almost unendurable loss when the Prophet Joseph Smith was martyred at Carthage Jail, sealing his work with his blood.

So it was that those early Saints were acquainted with loss.

Yet a unique kind of loss swept over the women who were left behind when the men of the Mormon Battalion marched away. Gone was not only their means of provision and protection, but the emotional and spiritual support these women had come to rely on in their marriages. It was as though all means of support and survival dissipated as husbands and sons disappeared over the horizon. Loneliness was mocked by prairie winds, howling wolves, and hovering uncertainties.

President Brigham Young's prophetic promise that no men would be killed in the combat of war was miraculously fulfilled, but some men did perish from other causes while separated from their families. Further bereavement resulted from the harsh reality of the death of children, who were overcome by starvation, disease, and exposure to the elements.

Dealing with heartrending losses and faced with the constant possibility of further loss, the women left behind by the Mormon Battalion turned to the Lord. Faith and doubt, questions and hopes paced back and forth in the hearts of the sisters until they arrived at their deepest communion with their Savior.

* * *

For your prayers have entered into the ears of the Lord of Sabaoth,
and are recorded with this seal and testament—
the Lord hath sworn and decreed that they be granted.

Therefore, he giveth this promise unto you,
with an immutable covenant that they shall be fulfilled,
and all things wherewith you have been afflicted shall work together
for your good,
and to my name's glory, saith the Lord.
—D&C 93:2–3

Margaret Robison Phelps

No eye to witness my sufferings but the pitying one of God—
He did not desert me.

MARGARET ROBISON WAS JUST SIXTEEN years old when she married
Alva Phelps in November 1835 in Susquehanna County, Pennsylvania. Both accepted the gospel before moving to Indiana and then on
to Nauvoo in 1843, where they witnessed the alarming aggression
of those who indiscriminately destroyed the homes and property of
Church members. Fearing for their lives and safety, Margaret and Alva
took their two children and fled Nauvoo, settling in Council Bluffs,
Iowa, where they were making plans to journey west.

In a letter to Sergeant Daniel Tyler, Margaret describes how their
plans were interrupted by the call to enlist in the battalion:

> We were traveling when the call came for him to leave us.
> It was nightfall when we were awakened from our slumbers
> with the painful news that we were to be left homeless, with-
> out a protector. I was very ill at the time, my children all
> small, my babe also extremely sick; but the call was pressing;
> there was no time for any provision to be made for wife or
> children; no time for tears; regret was unavailing. He started
> in the morning. I watched him from my wagon-bed till his
> loved form was lost in the distance. (Tyler, 129–130)

Two months later, Margaret heard rumors that a few members of
the battalion were returning to Iowa for their families and that her

husband was among them. The news was a welcome relief; with her limited means, she began to prepare for his homecoming.

In brighter spirits, Margaret attended her Sunday church meeting. As she sat in the congregation, nothing could have prepared her for the startling public announcement: "Our hearts go out in sympathy to Sister Phelps this morning due to the death of her husband" (Maynes, 369–370). Shocked and disoriented, Margaret gathered her skirts, rose from her seat, stumbled to the door, and fainted on the threshold. She later wrote, "This blow entirely prostrated me. But I had just embarked on my sea of troubles" (Tyler, 130).

Margaret was now alone with two small children and was expecting her third. At first she took great courage when her brother William promised to care for her, but when William fell victim to cholera, Margaret found herself in the most dire of circumstances. Her poignant account of her winter privation ends with a personal recognition of her faith in God:

> Winter found me bed-ridden and destitute, in a wretched hovel which was built on a hill-side; the season was one of constant rain; the situation of the hovel and its openness gave free access to piercing winds, and water flowed over the dirt floor, converting it into mud two or three inches deep; no wood but what my little ones picked up around the fences, so green it filled the room with smoke; the rain dripping and wetting the bed which I was powerless to leave; no relative to cheer or comfort me, a stranger away from all who ever loved me; my neighbors could do but little, their own troubles and destitution engrossing their time; my little daughter of seven my only help; no eye to witness my sufferings but the pitying one of God—He did not desert me. (Tyler, 130)

It would have been tragic enough for Margaret to learn that her husband had been cut down in battle or perished at the hand of an enemy; but when she later learned the circumstances surrounding her husband's death, the loss must have been almost impossible to reconcile:

Alva Phelps, of Company "E" died, a martyr to his country and religion. It is understood that he begged Dr. Sanderson not to give him any strong medicine, as all he needed was a little rest and then he would return to duty. But the doctor prepared his dose and ordered him to take it, which he declined doing; whereupon, the doctor, with some horrid oaths, forced it down him with the "old rusty spoon." A few hours later he died. The general feeling was that the doctor had killed him. . . . (Tyler, 158)

For Margaret, the circumstances of that "long, dreary winter" were slow to improve. As she later reflected on those months, she wrote, "I thank the Lord this was the darkest part of my life" (Tyler, 130).

Two years later, Margaret remarried and made the journey west, arriving in the Salt Lake Valley in October 1851. She settled with her family in Fillmore until the death of her husband, after which she moved to Oakley, Idaho, to live with one of her daughters. She passed away March 3, 1892.

* * *

Master, with anguish of spirit I bow in my grief today.
The depths of my sad heart are troubled. Oh waken and save, I pray!
Torrents of sin and of anguish Sweep o'er my sinking soul,
And I perish! I perish! Dear Master. Oh, hasten and take control.

Master the terror is over. The elements sweetly rest.
Earth's sun in the calm lake is mirrored, And heaven's within my breast.
Linger, O blessed Redeemer! Leave me alone no more,
And with joy I shall make the blest harbor, And rest on the blissful shore.

—Hymns, *105; lyrics, Mary Ann Baker, 1874*

Sarah Beriah Fiske Allen Ricks

*I desired that my life might be pure and that I might
have a right to the tree of life.*

IN HER JOURNAL, SARAH BERIAH FISKE described Ezra H. Allen as a "person of good character." On Christmas Day 1837, they were married (Sarah Allen Journal [SA], 1). Just a few years into their marriage, the couple attended a meeting in a schoolhouse where two Mormon missionaries delivered a message about a "golden Bible." Sarah wrote:

> After the opening, a quiet and unassuming man arose and said that he had not come to preach any new doctrine, but that the doctrine was old. (The same that Jesus and his apostles taught when He was upon the earth.) I felt that his remarks were reasonable and well sustained by quotations from the scriptures. My friends asked what I thought of the preaching. I said I couldn't condemn the scriptures. (SA, 1)

When Sarah's husband and two brothers decided to be baptized, she wrote concerning the desire for her own inner convictions to be clarified:

> I sought the silent recesses of my chamber and poured out my soul to the Lord. I besought Him not to suffer me in my weakness to reject the truth, but if the doctrines I heard were from Him, and were principles of life and salvation, that I might receive them. My mind was occupied in meditation, praying and reading. (SA, 1)

When Ezra was baptized a few months later, Sarah was not able to attend because of her need to maintain strict watchcare over an extremely sick daughter. Ezra returned home with the elders after his baptism, asking the missionaries to give their sick baby girl a blessing. In a sorrowing declaration of faith in a gospel she was struggling to embrace, Sarah wrote, "Our infant was blessed but not healed. Our Heavenly Father had decreed it to be otherwise and its blessed spirit was freed" (SA, 2).

After the death of their infant daughter, a concerned Ezra decided to take his family to join the Saints in Illinois. In 1843, the Allen family was living in Shocoquan, about twenty-five miles up the Mississippi River from Nauvoo. It was in this idyllic surrounding that the couple was blessed with a son. Sarah recounted the events surrounding the birth of her baby boy:

> We named him Alexander Hamilton. When he was a few days old I requested my husband to raise me up in bed to a sitting position. He did this and sat upon the side of the bed supporting me in his arms. Our new babe lay upon my lap.
>
> As we sat gazing upon his innocent healthy face, suddenly three drops of [Sarah's husband's] blood fell upon my hand and sleeve. I was still weak, nervous and frightened, but my husband soothed my fears and wiped away the blood. I again became calm.
>
> Soon after my husband was seized with chills and fever and in a few days our little daughter came running into the house shivering from head to foot. "Oh, Mama, it is so cold. It is going to rain," and climbed upon my bed. I covered her where she lay chilling until the fever came. In a few days I too was attacked with the ague. We were now a family of invalids. It was difficult to hire a nurse on account of so much sickness all around us. I had to be my own nurse. (SA, 3)

As she struggled through her own pain and sickness, endeavoring to restore her family's health, Sarah watched her new babe, Alexander, pass away after only eight weeks of life. Her journal revealed that the entire family was then taken with a debilitating disease and that "A few of my kind friends came in and prepared my baby for burial. There was not anyone of my family able to accompany it to the grave" (SA, 3).

Sarah's journal describes how her own illness worsened:

> I grew weaker, one disease after another setting in until I
> fainted and became unconscious. I was believed by all who
> saw me, to be dying. I remained in this condition two nights
> and one day. Suddenly I became conscious but was too weak
> to move, speak or open my eyes. Several persons in the house
> remarked that 'Sister Allen is dying.' I heard them remark
> about my general character and the esteem they held for me.
> One woman whispered in my ear and sent a message to a
> friend who had passed beyond.
>
> Later a lady came in and asked how long I had lain in
> that condition and if they had given me any nourishment.
> She then mixed some wine and water and with a teaspoon
> put a few drops in my mouth. It ran out as I had not the
> power to swallow it. She then put the spoon down to the
> root of my tongue and got a few drops to run down my
> throat. I then began to receive a little strength. She contin-
> ued until I could swallow, then I put out my tongue and
> touched my lips. She sent for meat broth and fed me. Thus
> as an angel of mercy she nursed me back to life. (SA, 3)

When Sarah and her family recovered, she earnestly desired to join
the body of the Saints in Nauvoo. Ezra granted her wish, and the family moved to "the city beautiful," where their every intention was to
work and live joyfully in a peaceful, permanent residence. But when
they were forced to leave their Nauvoo home in April 1846 and began
traveling west, news reached Ezra that a call had been issued for five
hundred men to join the Mormon Battalion. Feeling he should join,
he situated Sarah at a temporary location at a place called Musketo
near Mount Pisgah, and then he continued on alone.

At least he *thought* he was alone. He did not realize that Sarah's cow
was following him down the path. In Sarah's eyes, the precious source
of milk for her and her two children was vanishing. She wrote:

> After [Ezra] had been gone a few hours my cow became
> determined to follow. She broke through the corral and
> ran after them. I could not leave my babe and little girl to

follow her. Overcome with desolation I wept bitter tears. I determined to go to a distant camp for help and found a young woman to stay with me. After my return in the evening much to my surprise I saw my cow come walking into camp. The Lord always provides for those who put their trust in him. (SA, 4)

Once Ezra arrived in Winter Quarters, he made arrangements for provisions to be sent back to Sarah—but the supplies never reached her. Destitute and unable to assemble the necessary resources to leave, Sarah remained in her small shanty in Musketo—initially meant only as a temporary shelter. Eventually, as all the other settlers moved away, leaving the area completely deserted, her only company was her children and her cow.

Throughout the long inclement winter, Sarah was sustained by a faith that generated an unflinching determination to preserve her family. Finally, in the spring of 1848, she began to prepare for Ezra's return:

The Lord had blessed my efforts to provide for my family and the Saints had been kind to me. A long journey lay before me and I looked forward to when his strong arms would lift these burdens of care. I gathered grapes from the lowlands near the river and made wine and prepared dainties that would please him. At length the news came that a company of Brethren was expected to cross the river in a few days. Circumstances wouldn't permit me to go to the ferry to meet them so I remained home waiting and listening to the sound of every footstep that approached my door. (SA, 5)

Then the news arrived. There would be no homecoming. Ezra and two other men had been slain in the Sierra Nevada Mountains at a place that would later come to be known as Tragedy Springs.

The circumstances surrounding Ezra's death are particularly fearsome and eventually became part of the history of pioneers who were accustomed to sacrifice. In that spring of 1848, Daniel Browett, Henderson Cox, and Sarah's husband, Ezra, decided to go ahead of the company as scouts in an effort to find an easier passage through the Sierra Nevada

Mountains. When the three men did not return in a reasonable time, concerned comrades went searching for them.

Sergeant Daniel Tyler described the scene where the three men were found:

> After turning out their stock and gathering around the spring to quench their thirst, some one picked up a blood-stained arrow, and after a little search other bloody arrows were also found. . . . Blood on rocks was also discovered, and a leather purse with gold dust in it was picked up and recognized as having belonged to Brother [Ezra] Allen. The worst fears . . . that the three missing pioneers had been murdered, were soon confirmed. A short distance from the spring they found a place about eight feet square, where the earth had lately been removed, and upon digging therein they found the dead bodies of their beloved brothers. . . . Their bodies were stripped naked, terribly mutilated and all buried in one shallow grave.
>
> The company buried them again and placed over their grave a large pile of rock, in a square form, as a monument to mark their last resting place, and shield them from the wolves. (Tyler, 337)

We do not know how much detail of the sad event fell on Sarah's ears, but she wrote in her journal of the day she received the news that her husband would not return:

> Thus were my hopes blasted in a moment. What could I do now but trust in God? I had no relatives in the church, two small children and a journey of a thousand miles before me. I felt as if I would sink under my burden of grief and anguish of heart. Then I aroused myself and began to meditate on what course to pursue, how to provide for my family and prepare for the journey. I determined to make every effort to accomplish this undertaking and leave the events in the hands of God. In a few days the purse which had been found containing the gold belonging to my husband was brought to me. There were marks of blood upon it which seemed to be the price of his life. (SA, 5)

Ezra's last gift to Sarah—the bloodstained pouch filled with gold dust mined at an awful price—became her salvation. Sarah traded the gold dust for cash and supplies for her journey west, keeping only enough gold to make two rings, which she wore in memory of her husband (see SA, 6).

Sarah took her two children westward to the Salt Lake Valley in 1852, where she worked as a school teacher and a "spinner of wool."

Later, she remarried and resided in Logan until her death at seventy-two years of age.

Giving Loved Ones to the Will of the Lord

WOMEN THROUGHOUT THE EARLY PERIOD of the Church made extraordinary sacrifices when relinquishing their husbands to the will of the Lord. While loss is often associated with defeat, bereavement, or hurt, giving to the Lord is never a loss; it is a sanctifying surrender. The women who gave their husbands to the Lord gave their own hearts and love to the power and glory of the Lord.

Mary Bingham Freeman lost her first husband, Elijah Norman Freeman, to the battalion. Her second husband, Willard Snow, later died while serving a mission in Denmark (see Maynes, 208, 209).

When Lois Coon Stevens heard that President Brigham Young was calling for men to enlist in the battalion, she knew that her stalwart companion of seventeen years would volunteer. Realizing she would be left alone, she hung her head in despair. Her husband, Arnold Stevens, died on the battalion march. She probably could never have imagined the further heartache that awaited her when death later claimed three more of her husbands (see Maynes, 456).

An account left to us by the hand of James Ferguson tells the story of Wealthy Richards, mother of Joseph W. Richards, a soldier who died on the battalion march at Pueblo, Colorado, November 21, 1846:

> There was one scene that was particularly touching. An aged mother, to whom the call of the government and the wish of the President were made known, came forward. She had five sons—one was murdered and now lay buried deep in the tragic well in Missouri. Two were in a foreign land preaching the faith for which their brother's blood was shed; one was

still too young . . . and needed care and comfort. The other was a young man, the sentinel and protector of her tottering steps. Even in her aged heart, withered and broken as it was, the love of country burned deep and strong. She yielded up her son and never saw him more. (Ricketts, 2)

Ann Ratcliff Karren

*Her oldest son, twelve years old, built a box of rough boards
and buried his baby sister.*

ANN'S LOVE STORY BEGAN IN a bakery in Lancashire, England, where she learned the art of baking from her father, who mentored her in every aspect of the business. When typhoid fever took his life, Ann inherited the sizable bakery. Finding herself overwhelmed by the strenuous workload, she advertised for a reliable assistant; a gentleman by the name of Mr. Thomas Karren, trained in "plain and fancy cooking," responded. Ann reviewed his recommendations, assessed his skills, and hired him (Maynes, 307).

Dusted with flour as they refined recipes for both "plain and fancy" delicacies of taste, Ann and Thomas industriously worked together side by side for two years before realizing their desire to spend the rest of their lives together.

When Thomas asked Ann's mother for permission to marry Ann, he was confronted with hostility and resentment. Ann's mother, Lydia, felt that there were irreconcilable religious differences; Thomas belonged to the Church of England, and Ann was a devout Catholic. Ann's grandmother, however, saw in Thomas a man who was trustworthy and would treat her granddaughter well. She intervened and the couple was married on May 11, 1833. The bakery business grew, and Ann and Thomas were able to purchase a beautiful home for their young family.

Thomas was by nature a very religious man and listened attentively when missionaries from The Church of Jesus Christ of Latter-day

Saints arrived in the area. After diligent study of the Book of Mormon, Thomas felt confident that he had found true doctrine. But Ann remained skeptical. And while the idea of accepting a new religion did not come easily to her, she nonetheless could not help but be inspired by the depth of her husband's commitment. For that reason she listened to the missionaries with an open heart and was baptized two months later.

Energized by a new vision of destiny, Thomas was eager to travel to Nauvoo, meet the Prophet Joseph Smith, and live among the Saints. Ann, on the other hand, had no interest in leaving her family, her friends, her bakery, or her country. Thomas was quiet but resolute.

Then one day, without warning or announcement, Ann single-mindedly purchased all the trunks, clothing, and basic provisions needed for the voyage across the ocean. Thomas was elated, and plans fell into place.

Leaving England proved to be the first in a chain of faith-testing events in Ann's life. The couple's youngest son, two-year-old Joseph, contracted diphtheria and died on the day of their departure. Boarding the ship bound for America, a grief-stricken Ann left her little boy with her sister to be buried.

Moreover, Ann was pregnant with her sixth child as she watched her hometown of Liverpool disappear behind the ocean's horizon. Brokenhearted by little Joseph's death and despairing of the very will to live, she fell ill at sea. But Thomas and their four children refused to let her yield to the despair that permeated her heart, and their support sustained her through the cheerless ocean passage.

Once settled in Nauvoo, Ann embarked on her new way of life. Participation in church meetings and activities rejuvenated her hopes. The family met Joseph Smith, and the Prophet's spirit—never lagging in spite of great adversity—inspired her. Nauvoo became her beloved home. Ann had come to feel that she had traded the moorlands of England for the tranquility of a gospel community, but, as for many of the Saints who had hoped to rest permanently within the quiet borders of Nauvoo, a fragile peace ruptured into a tumultuous uproar. Thomas and Ann were endowed in the Nauvoo Temple on February 3, 1846, one day before fleeing with the Saints across the frozen Mississippi River.

Lengthening Ann's chain of sacrifice, Thomas decided to depart with the Mormon Battalion. Listening to the counsel of President

Brigham Young, Thomas obeyed and enlisted. He wrote: "Only the strongest sense of duty and devotion to my religion could induce me to leave my wife in her delicate condition and our children under such distressing conditions" (Maynes, 310).

Thomas may or may not have known just how "delicate" Ann's condition would prove to be. Pregnant when Thomas enlisted, the shock at his leaving caused her to give birth prematurely. The baby girl, also named Ann, lived for only a single day. Laying ill in a wagon box, Ann was so weak that she could not attend the funeral of her newborn. Her oldest son, John, a mere twelve years of age, built a box of rough boards and buried his baby sister. It was the second time Ann was unable to attend to the burial of one of her children.

The rainy season was unrelenting, and Ann found herself still living in the wagon box during the wettest part of the year. The threadbare cover for the wagon proved incapable of repelling water, and Ann found herself, along with her bedding and clothing, completely immersed every morning. In an attempt to help their mother, her three oldest children—John, twelve, Catherine, ten, and Lydia, eight—lifted her up, dipped the water out from underneath her, and laid her back down (see Maynes, 310).

When Ann's health was finally restored, a kind man passing through Council Bluffs made her a charitable offer. He had just vacated his cabin in Garden Grove, Iowa, and told Ann that she and the children could live there. She accepted the offer; at last she and her family had a roof over their heads and a plot of land on which to grow food. Ann spent her time cultivating a garden and selling her extra produce, earning "several hundred dollars" from her potatoes (see Maynes, 310).

Thomas returned to Iowa in October 1847 wearing a buckskin coat and shoes stitched in buffalo hide. His shaggy appearance terrified his younger children—but when finally reacquainted, the little ones were joyously animated by the presence of their long-absent father. (see Maynes, 311).

Preparing to follow the Saints west, Thomas and Ann opened a new bakery in order to raise money for the trek; Ann made the cakes and pies while Thomas baked the bread and crackers. Employing their keen business sense and hard work ethic, the Karren family was prepared for their journey west by June 1850.

After settling in the Salt Lake Valley, Thomas received a mission call to the Sandwich Islands. Perhaps recalling the privations and perilous conditions that persisted during his absence with the battalion, Ann was overcome with fear at the thought of her husband's departure to a faraway land. Again she lay ill, this time infected with mountain fever. President George A. Smith visited her home and gave her a blessing, promising that her health would be restored if she would be at peace with her husband's voyage. Reaching into an inner reservoir of faith that not even she may have known she possessed, she consented to the call.

Thomas fulfilled an honorable three-year mission. Upon his return, he found Ann and his children safe and healthy. The Karren family remained in Utah, actively involved in religious and community affairs (see Maynes, 311).

The Giving of Life

ALTHOUGH THE NUMBER OF INFANTS who died in Iowa seemed too great to be counted, a numerical sum would eventually be assigned to the many tiny bodies that lay in hastily dug graves. Yet it would truly be impossible to calculate the impact on the hearts of the women who left those graves behind alongside the "trail of tears."

Children passed away at an alarming rate. Colonel Thomas L. Kane wrote:

> Here at one time the digging got behind; burials were slow; and you might see women sit in the open tents keeping the flies off their dead children, sometime after decomposition had set in. (Howe, 428)

Births were precarious. Women gave birth in wagon boxes, in dug-outs, and sometimes in nothing more than the prairie grass. Often the only shield of protection and privacy offered to the birthing mother was the fabric of skirts held in the hands of the sisters who encircled her.

DOULA SUN

We have no homes of brick and stone and earth and wood
Wherein we sisters might labor
To bring God's children into the world.

As we travel west
It feels so inadequate sometimes,

But Moses reminds us that

As Israel traveled west
They had no house of brick and stone and earth and wood
In which to bring God into the world.

So they set up walls of cloth
And called it a tabernacle
And God called it home.

When walls of cloth are all we have,
Then they will serve to enclose God's daughters
As they labor
To bring God's children
Into the world.

—Dane Laverty, 2005

TRIUMPH

My son, peace be unto thy soul; thine adversity and thine affictions shall be but a small moment: And then if thou endure it well, God shall exalt thee on high; thou shalt triumph over all thy foes. —D&C 121:7–8

THE PROMISE TO THE PROPHET JOSEPH—and to all of us—is the promise of triumph over *all* foes. Of the foes to be conquered, there are those that assail from without and those that strike from within. Some of the most formidable foes for those of any age are the ones embedded deep inside the heart. Certainly such was the case for the men and women who left all they knew behind and set off for the unknown across an inhospitable and endless wilderness.

The women who made the journey cultivated a triumphant will as they conquered the practical foes of survival—such as the woman who rose to the occasion and trained the cows to pull her wagon when her team of oxen was taken away by a captain of one of the companies. But the greater victory was the conquest of spirit in refusing to be shackled by spiritual impairments—like the natural tendency to hold a grudge against the man who had unjustly pirated the oxen.

Stretched to the nethermost extreme by physical hardship and disappointment, these prairie refugees recognized that forgiveness and cooperation were the keys to survival, protection, and happiness. In the battle for survival, the greatest triumphs were the triumphs of the spirit.

The stories of these women readily demonstrate that they did not spend time lamenting over circumstances that could not be altered.

Instead, they moved "onward"—often alone—and their cast-iron resolve brought them to triumph.

The forbearance and long-suffering of their afflictions brought them not only to the free space of the vast Rocky Mountains but also to the free space of inner spiritual freedoms such as love, trust, self-confidence, self-reliance, forgiveness, faith, and hope. Step by step, prayer by prayer, the pioneers journeyed. They continued onward until, sometimes on this side of the veil but most often on His side, they were able to see the wide and far-reaching scope of their triumph.

Catherine Ann Williams Owens

A woman would only be a nuisance to the company.

CATHERINE ANN WILLIAMS'S CHILDHOOD DID not begin with optimistic prospects. Her mother passed away soon after she was born, and two cousins subsequently took her in. When it became clear that her environment was ruled by meanness and brutality, her grandmother rode a hundred miles on a mule to come to her rescue, provide a new home, and offer new hope.

At eighteen years of age, Catherine Ann married Robert Owens. Seven years after their wedding, Robert joined the Church, and Catherine was baptized one year later. Deeply converted to the gospel, they humbly named their infant son after the Book of Mormon prophet Nephi.

In February 1846, just days before fleeing Nauvoo, Catherine and Robert were endowed in the Nauvoo Temple. On the morning of their icy river crossing, Catherine was five months into her fifth pregnancy.

Requesting enlistments, the battalion call sounded as Catherine and Robert reached Mount Pisgah. Supportive of Robert's decision to enlist, Catherine felt secure and well equipped to care for her family—Robert had diligently provided her with all necessary supplies for the journey west, including her most valuable asset, a team of finely trained oxen. As Catherine watched Robert disappear over the horizon with the other soldiers, she was confident she would be traveling with one of the first companies leaving for the Salt Lake Valley.

But her confidence was confronted by unforeseen trials.

Four weeks after Robert marched away, little Mary Elizabeth was born but did not live. Then Catherine's two other daughters, four-year-old Isabelle and six-year-old Josephine, were overcome by diphtheria. It was with tears in her eyes that Catherine rebuilt her fortitude and will.

Now left with only her two sons, four-year-old Nephi and nine-year-old Jerome, Catherine engaged all of her energy in arranging final preparations for the westward trek. At that point one of the captains walked up to Catherine, took her team of trained oxen away from her, and said, "A woman would only be a nuisance to the company" (Maynes, 354).

Refusing defeat, Catherine's physical and spiritual stamina brought her to triumph as she assessed her situation and redetermined to make the journey west. Leveraging what little she had left, Catherine trained two *cows* to pull her wagon and, with her two little boys in tow, traveled with the John Lowry Company, arriving in the Salt Lake Valley in the fall of 1847.

Catherine possessed a resilience and clear-mindedness that resurfaced repeatedly throughout her life, as aptly demonstrated on one particular occasion during her journey west: Each morning she poured the day's extra milk into a "dash" that she hung on the bouncing wagon; the movement of the wagon throughout the day churned the milk into butter. One day when her animals became spooked and stampeded, Catherine quickly and instinctively grabbed the reigns of her team and was holding on for dear life as she levelheadedly yelled back to Jerome, "Hold on to the churn dash!" (Maynes, 354).

When Robert returned to Utah after being released from the service, he took a second wife, Martha Evins Allen. Both Catherine and Martha were sealed to Robert by Heber C. Kimball.

At a general conference on August 28, 1852, Robert was one of ninety-eight men whose names were read from the pulpit as being called to serve a mission. There had been no forewarning. Robert left within days for the India-Australia Mission. Catherine and Martha, both pregnant at the time, darned his socks, mended and scrubbed his frayed shirts, patched his worn coat, and made a new suit for him from "homespun."

The parting counsel Robert gave to Catherine was representative of the faith of the early Saints and is instructive for us in our day: "Trust in the Lord and never doubt His watchful care over us, all will be well" (Maynes, 356).

AFTER THE BATTALION:
MORE WAITING, MORE TRAVELING

THE BATTALION'S DAUNTING MARCH TO California and the Saints' long trek to the Salt Lake Valley did not mark the end of traveling and parting, of waiting and relocating. For the hardy members of the early Church, there were still arduous journeys ahead and periods of separation to be endured.

Some were called to serve missions, and many were involved in colonization. An uninterrupted existence of ease and tranquility was not the destiny for most of those who arrived in the Salt Lake Valley at the end of a toilsome westward migration.

Many of the soldiers returning from the battalion march were called to serve missions that again took them away from their families, often for three years at a time.

Additionally, expansive colonization required that many of the Saints relocate as often as two or three times after reaching Utah. President Brigham Young led the colonization of a stretch of land known as Deseret that covered a vast area of the West, including all of present-day Utah, most of Nevada and Arizona, and parts of Oregon, Idaho, Wyoming, Colorado, New Mexico, California, and an area across the border into Mexico. Hard work built and energized the land that was settled and developed into communities, farms, and industries.

Many battalion families—such as that of Sarah Ann Arterbury Church and her husband, Haden—were both missionaries and colonizers. Haden Wells Church served three missions; his first mission, where he labored in Alabama and Tennessee, was completed before his enlistment in the battalion. After his service in the battalion was fulfilled, he served his second mission in Great Britain; he served a third mission again in the United States.

At the completion of Haden's third mission, President Brigham Young asked him and Sarah to leave the Salt Lake Valley and rebuild in St. George, where they were to promote the cotton industry in the Dixie Mission. Recognizing that such relocation would challenge not only the men who had marched with the battalion and served missions throughout the world, but also their wives—who had demonstrated unparalleled valor in protecting and providing for their families in the absence of their husbands—the prophet directly addressed this counsel to the women:

> President Young told the people to consider their mission to raise cotton as important to them as if they were preaching the gospel to the people of the earth. He told the "wives to go with their husbands in the spirit of joy, cheerfulness, and feel pleasure in going." (Maynes, 118)

* * *

It may not be on the mountain height
Or over the stormy sea,
It may not be on the battle's front
My Lord will have need of me.
But, if by a still small voice he calls
To paths that I do not know,
I'll answer, dear Lord, with my hand in thine:
I'll go where you want me to go.

—Hymns, *270; lyrics, Mary Brown, 1856–1918*

Kiziah Brown Hunter

She carried single-shot cap-and-ball pistols in each of her apron pockets, one on either side.

KIZIAH BROWN AND JESSE DIVINED HUNTER married in St. Louis, Missouri, in December 1827, amidst a particularly fierce upheaval of hostile persecutions. In 1838, while the Saints were meeting with the militia under truce to settle the Missouri disputations, Church members were taken captive. In the hands of a dangerous and unpredictable mob-like militia, eighty Mormon men were dragged to the public square. Joseph Smith described the scene:

> We, after much entreaty, were suffered to see our families, being attended all the while by a strong guard. I found my wife and children in tears, who feared we had been shot by those who had sworn to take our lives, and that they would see us no more. When I entered my house, they clung to my garments, their eyes streaming with tears, while mingled emotions of joy and sorrow were manifested in their countenances. . . .
>
> Who can realize the feelings which I experienced at that time, to be thus torn from my companion, and leave her surrounded with monsters in the shape of men. . . . My partner wept, my children clung to me, until they were thrust from me by the swords of the guards. I felt overwhelmed while I witnessed the scene. (Joseph Smith, 193)

In the confrontation, Jesse was taken prisoner alongside the Prophet Joseph Smith and a number of other men (see Joseph Smith, 187–188). A helpless Kiziah could do no more than watch.

After stripping the Mormon community of all weapons, pillaging personal belongings, and laying even worse offenses on the Mormon community, the state militia's commanding officer, Samuel Lucas, delivered the men to General Clark for court-martial. The words of Parley P. Pratt convey the Saints' indignation:

> What! Ministers of the gospel tried by court martial! Men who sustain no office in military affairs, and who are not subject by law to military duty; such men to be tried by court martial! And this in time of peace, and in a republic where the constitution guaranteed to every citizen the right of trial by jury? (Pratt, 198–199)

Following the court-martial, Samuel Lucas issued the following order:

> To Brigadier General Doniphan,
> Sir:—You will take Joseph Smith and the other prisoners into the public square of Far West, and shoot them at 9 o'clock tomorrow morning. Signed, Samuel D. Lucas, Major General Commanding. (Joseph Smith, 190)

General Doniphan replied:

> It is cold-blooded murder. I will not obey your order. My brigade shall march for Liberty tomorrow morning at 8 o'clock; and if you execute these men, I will hold you responsible before an earthy tribunal, so help me God. Signed, A. W. Doniphan, Brigadier-General. (Joseph Smith, 190–191)

Jesse and the other prisoners were then marched to Jackson County as their helpless wives and children looked on.

According to Parley P. Pratt, Joseph Smith delivered a comforting, prophetic promise of safety just as the journey began:

> As we arose and commenced our march on the morning
> of November 3, Joseph Smith spoke to me and the other
> prisoners, in a low, but cheerful and confidential tone; said
> he: "Be of good cheer, brethren; the word of the Lord came
> to me last night that our lives should be given us, and that
> whatever we may suffer during this captivity, not one of our
> lives should be taken." Of this prophecy I testify in the name
> of the Lord, and, though spoken in secret, its public fulfill-
> ment and the miraculous escape of each one of us is too
> notorious to need my testimony. (Pratt, 192)

Kiziah was obviously not aware of the prophecy guaranteeing safety
for the prisoners, and she watched powerlessly as mobs and militia vied
for the opportunity to harm the Mormon men of the community. When
the men were marched away to Richmond, again she could do nothing
more than wait. For Kiziah, as for many of the pioneer women, waiting
was often her triumph.

Eventually, the prisoners were arraigned before Judge Austin A.
King in Richmond. Parley P. Pratt described the proceeding as a

> mock Court of Inquiry [where] the Judge could not be pre-
> vailed on to examine the conduct of murderers and robbers
> who had desolated our society, nor would he receive testi-
> mony except against us. By the dissenters and apostates who
> wished to save their own lives and secure their property at
> the expense of others, and by those who had murdered and
> plundered us from time to time, he obtained abundance of
> testimony, much of which was entirely false. (Pratt, 211)

After the trial, Jesse was dismissed along with most of the other
men; Joseph Smith and five other Church leaders were imprisoned in
Liberty Jail on false charges of treason (see Pratt, 214).

Jesse, free to return to his family, was understandably concerned
about the Prophet and the continuing persecution but must have
hoped that the Saints would prevail and eventually find security and
peace. Two years later, Jesse and Kiziah must have felt at least a glimmer
of that hope as they peacefully settled in Nauvoo, where the Prophet
was then residing.

But the security for which they longed again evaded them. A short six years later, in 1846, Jesse and his family were among the exiled Saints who hastily fled across the icy Mississippi River.

When the Hunter family reached Mount Pisgah, Jesse heard that men were needed for the Mormon Battalion; he decided to enlist as a soldier. Recognizing Jesse's leadership abilities, President Brigham Young selected him to serve as captain of Company B. Kiziah's sacrifice was yet increased when her sixteen-year-old son, William, accompanied his father on the march as a drummer for Company B (see Maynes, 278).

Both Jesse and William sent Kiziah money to buy supplies for her journey west. Kiziah's astute management of her funds and other resources enabled her to equip herself and her five children for the trek. Though she had many of the provisions she needed for a successful journey—and certainly more than some of the families who set out on the trek—it is almost impossible to imagine the demands placed upon a woman who faced such a task on her own, without the benefits of physical, emotional, or spiritual support from a husband at her side.

But face it she did, and triumph she did. Kiziah and her children arrived safely in the Salt Lake Valley with the Captain Asa Barton Company on September 24, 1847.

Jesse was discharged from the battalion on July 16, 1847, but before he could return to Utah, he was appointed by Governor Mason to be the Indian Agent in Upper California. He was charged with the responsibility "to guard all property belonging to the mission, to give protection to all the Indians living at the mission and in the neighborhood, and make rules for governing the Indians" (Maynes, 279–280).

Not wanting to be separated from her husband any longer, Kiziah once again packed up her family and made the long desert trek from Utah to California. Once again she drove the wagon and team by herself. Worried about tales she had heard of dangers on the trail, she carried single-shot cap-and-ball pistols in her apron pockets, one on either side. On one occasion when her wagon was attacked, she discharged her ammunition, shooting a man in the leg (see Maynes, 280).

Despite arming herself and preparing for every other possible contingency that she could envision on her journey to California, Kiziah encountered an unexpected danger when her two redheaded sons were kidnapped by Paiute Indians. When found, both boys were calmly eating stew, surrounded by a quiet band of Indians who were fascinated with their fiery red hair. After the Indians pulled out some hair to keep, the boys were safely returned to Kiziah (see Maynes, 280).

Kiziah's talents and hopes were threaded together with an indomitable will. Despite malicious persecutions and the challenges of traveling alone with her children across vast miles of difficult terrains, Kiziah triumphed. And despite waiting through moments of severe anxiety during the endangerment of her husband, Kiziah prevailed.

If not at first obvious, both Jesse and Kiziah triumphed in serving the US government, reconciling feelings of anger and bitterness toward a government that had shown injustice and evasion of duty.

Kiziah and Jesse eventually built their family life in California, becoming part of the colonization of San Bernardino. Living out their lives among other former Battalion comrades, they enjoyed the fruits of lifelong friendships as they witnessed the expansion of the West.

The Fury of Persecution

What kind of fury has set itself upon this earth?
It is the blackest storm, with predatory winds
That shred bone from its marrow.
Its jagged jaws and teeth
Draw blood from trust, faith, and possibility.
It is the voracious appetite for ignorance that will justify its power,
And it is the craving of darkness wherein lies
Comfort of self-gluttonous concealment.

Some winds have passed.
It is quieter now.
But the dark winds have just become more
Secretive.

—C. Prohosky

PATRIOTISM:

 # THE RAISING OF THE AMERICAN FLAG

ONGOING PERSECUTION HAD BELEAGUERED THE Saints almost from the time the Church was organized, and the government had woefully failed in protecting both the liberty and lives of those who had embraced the gospel. Despite what appeared to be a constant miscarriage of justice, one of the greatest triumphs of the Mormon community was the sense of patriotism that managed to overtake deep-rooted resentments.

Most of the families that had been driven from Nauvoo had grandfathers and great-uncles who had fought in the Revolutionary War. It was not uncommon, in fact, for both maternal and paternal grandfathers to have been involved in the Revolution. A letter penned by George Taggart reads:

> I feel Fanny as though I had made as great a sacrifice as I could . . . in order to show that the Blood of my Grandfathers who fought and bled in the revolutionary war and the spirit of liberty and freedom still courses in the veins of some of their posterity that are called Mormons. . . . (Taggart Family Organization)

Because the enormous sacrifices made by the Saints' forefathers were so recent a part of their heritage, the price paid for freedom was personal and immediate to them. As a result, a deep love of country and a trust in the Constitution flowed through their veins, and when the government condoned the escalating persecutions, allowing and sometimes even encouraging injury and injustice, the Saints were left with intensified feelings of bewilderment and betrayal. Their loved ones had bled for a country that would not protect them.

Under these conditions and subject to bitter indignation at the realization that their country was now requesting even greater sacrifice—possibly the loss of yet more lives in the calamity of war—the Saints nonetheless responded in an extraordinarily patriotic manner to the raising of the American flag. Thomas L. Kane describes a scene of incomparable loyalty to God, to prophet, and to country:

> [The Saints] had twice been persuaded by (State) government authorities in Illinois and Missouri, to give up their arms on some special appeals to their patriotic confidence and had then been left to the malice of their enemies. And now they were asked, in the midst of the Indian country, to surrender over five hundred of their best men for a war-march of thousands of miles to California, without the hope of return until after the conquest of that country. Could they view such a proposition with favor? But the feeling of country triumphed . . . an American flag [was] brought out from the store-house of things rescued, and hoisted to the top of a tree mast—and, in three days, the force—five hundred and twenty in number, was reported, mustered, organized, and ready to march. (Howe 423–424)

The Mormon community had triumphed; the Saints would sacrifice on behalf of the Church, allowing funds to be generated for their families and for the westward trek. But perhaps just as crucial, the Saints would realize that their Heavenly Father desired that they remain an integral part of the American nation.

Emily Abbott Bunker

An expert with needle and cloth . . .

EMILY ABOTT BUNKER LEARNED OF the triumph of forgiveness and mercy.

Born into an affluent New York family, Emily Abbott was well educated in the finest schools and enjoyed a secure childhood during which she wanted for nothing. When she was ten, her family moved west to a forty-acre farm in Illinois. It was here that the Bunker family accepted the gospel and subsequently moved to Nauvoo.

Emily's father passed away when she was sixteen; to help support her mother and five brothers and sisters, Emily found employment as an apprentice to a tailor. Hard-working and skillful, she soon enjoyed a reputation as one of the finest seamstresses in Nauvoo (see Maynes, 86).

Three years later, Emily met Edward Bunker, who was immediately taken with her beauty. Their wedding ceremony was conducted by John Taylor on February 9, 1846, amidst the clamorous upheaval of the winter evacuation from Nauvoo.

When Edward and Emily reached Council Bluffs, they were without means for their journey west. The battalion call sounded, and military wages seemed the perfect solution. Edward enlisted.

Nineteen-year-old Emily was pregnant with their first child when Edward marched away, and she was destined to deliver her child in the bitter reach of February.

Following is an account of her life-changing experience:

Emily, an expert with needle and cloth, sometimes felt superior to those not dressed as well as she. One day [while living in Nauvoo] she saw a young baby dressed in some glazed curtain material. The material had bright shawl-type flower figures on a deep blue background. Curtain material for a baby dress she questioned? She criticized the mother for not being able to provide better and vowed out loud: "I would not clothe my child in a dress like that, even if I could have it for nothing." . . .

When on February 1, 1847, Emily gave birth to her baby boy, she had nothing to clothe him in. No one in camp had anything she could buy to sew into baby clothes. No one, that is, except the mother she had criticized for using curtain material. The mother kindly said to her: "I have yet a few yards of the same material from which I made my baby's dress. You are welcome to it." Emily, swallowing her pride, accepted the curtain material and offered to pay for it. "No, I don't want you to pay for it," the giver said. "I hope you need it so much that you'll not shed tears over it and blame the Lord because you have no better." Emily did not complain about the curtain cloth dress she made for her son. For a long time it was the only clothing the baby boy had. (Maynes, 87)

Edward returned to Winter Quarters in December 1847, one week before Christmas, where he was introduced to his first son, Edward Bunker Jr. This Christmas season must have been one of the most beautiful, lit by the brightness of jubilant reunion.

Emily always remembered not only the curtain material that clothed her son but also the kind lady who returned generosity for insult. Later, as the mother of eleven children, Emily would tell the story to her little ones to help them accept difficult situations when money and extras were lacking. Emily's triumph toward humility would be passed down to her children (see Maynes, 87).

This story of triumph would not be complete without remembering the unnamed woman who gave kindly and generously of her means after a hurtful assault of offense.

Kindness perpetuated triumph.

SACRIFICE

A SACRIFICE IS AN OFFERING that is freely given and that often expresses one's awareness of ~~his~~ duty to God. A deep manifestation of devotion and dedication, sacrifice is often accompanied by prayer, communicating a genuine gratitude to a loving Heavenly Father for life and its attendant blessings (see LDS Bible Dictionary, 766).

Sacrifices vary in intensity, requirement, and length of endurance.., Without doubt, the ultimate sacrifice is the offering of one's complete will to our God and our Savior. The words of a traditional Christian hymn express it well:

> *Come Dear Creator come,*
> *From thy bright heavenly throne*
> *Come take possession of our souls,*
> *And make them all thine own.*
>
> *—Hymns UK*

In surrendering their will to the Creator, some of the these women gave their lives to Him. Their offering—freely given—manifested an all-encompassing devotion to His purposes. Through their last and ultimate sacrifice, their testimonies were sealed for their posterity . . . and for us . . . forever.

* * *

And it shall come to pass that those who die in me shall not taste of death, for it shall be sweet unto them. —D&C 42:46

Nancy Reeder Walker Alexander

She would hug her husband's riding boots to her,
and weep . . .

NANCY REEDER WALKER WAS THE ninth of ten children in a family of early converts to the Church. One of a hard-working group of early Saints, Nancy grew up sharing in the labors of supporting her family. She regularly attended church meetings in Winchester, Indiana, where her faith grew.

By contrast, Horace Martin Alexander grew up in luxury, enjoying the wealth of Southern plantations that ornamented the landscapes of Virginia and Kentucky. Part of a family that relied on servants, he was not accustomed to manual labor. At nineteen, Horace struck out on his own and found himself in Indiana, where he joined a group of young men whose ambition it was to taunt and torment the Saints during church meetings.

It would appear that Nancy and Horace were an unlikely couple. But after becoming acquainted with the "devout Mormon girl, Nancy," Horace had a change of heart and was soon giving full attention the teachings of the gospel (see Horace Martin Alexander). He began attending Church meetings with Nancy and was eventually converted to the truthfulness of the gospel and to the Mormon way of life.

Nancy Reeder Walker and Horace Martin Alexander were married September 14, 1834; she was sixteen years of age, he twenty-two.

The newlyweds traveled to join the saints in Missouri. There they settled in Liberty and welcomed their first daughter, Frances Evelyn, into their family. Horace built a comfortable home and worked on his small farm. He was also a storekeeper in Far West and told stories about how the Prophet Joseph Smith, "an imposing man," would ride a white horse directly into the store, where the horse would indicate what Joseph wanted by pawing with his front leg in front of the desired item (see Horace Martin Alexander). Brigham Young ordained Horace an elder in the Church, and the future of the small family seemed one of prosperity and optimism (see Maynes, 23).

But all prospects of peace were obliterated when Governor Lilburn Boggs signed the "Extermination Order." Fearing that the members of the Church were too numerous and too prosperous, Missouri residents raised both voices and arms against the Saints. On October 27, 1838, giving way to mob belligerence, Governor Boggs issued his lethal mandate: "The Mormons must be treated as enemies, and must be exterminated or driven from the state" (see Extermination Order).

Nancy and Horace fled the state as quickly as possible with tiny Frances Evelyn clasped in their arms. Leaving all else behind, they camped on the muddy, mosquito-infested banks of the Mississippi River until they finally found refuge with sympathetic residents in Quincy, Illinois.

On April 6, 1841, at the general conference of the Church, the cornerstones of the Nauvoo Temple were laid. A call came from the Prophet Joseph Smith requesting that men skilled in carpentry donate their expertise to the building of the temple. Horace answered the call, and for the next few years, his family was peacefully settled in Nauvoo. Believing they had finally found a tranquil respite, Horace and Nancy continued to build their family, welcoming two more daughters.

But the darkening clouds of persecution again stalked the Saints, dismantling their dreams and expectations of a peaceful, worshipful life. When the Prophet and his brother were martyred, the Saints were counseled to begin preparations for evacuation. Nancy and Horace received their endowments in January and fled the city the following month.

When Brigham Young called for recruits for the Mormon Battalion, Horace enlisted. Now a private in Company B under Captain Jesse D. Hunter, he left his pregnant wife and three young daughters behind.

The prairie winter of 1846–1847 was bitter, blustery, and unrelenting; it was in that arctic climate that Nancy gave birth to her only son,

Horace Martin Alexander Jr. on January 1, 1847. The cabin in which they huddled together was cold and wet, and there was not sufficient bedding to keep Nancy and her baby warm and dry. Still suffering the effects of childbirth, Nancy developed pneumonia. A fifteen-year-old orphan, Catherine Housten, was sent to care for her, her infant son, and her three daughters. Catherine reported that Nancy, receding into inconsolable loneliness, often hugged Horace's riding boots to her chest and wept.

The son that was born to Nancy on New Year's Day should have heralded a lasting celebration. But the winds were too chilling, the snows were too deep, and Nancy was too weak.

On January 28, 1847, Nancy died. Three days later, her infant son, Horace Martin Alexander Jr., also died. Nancy's grave was reopened, and his tiny body was placed next to hers for burial. Deep in the earth they rested together, tempering each other from the cold.

Horace had felt uneasy about Nancy's welfare throughout his entire march with the battalion. From a compilation of Battalion soldiers' journals, we read:

> Friday, December 25, at Rainbow Valley, Arizona: "Horace Alexander worried about his wife. She was with child when he left in July and the baby was due about this time. He wondered if the baby was born and if he had a son or daughter." (Ricketts, 105)

> Sunday, May 30, San Diego: "When the mail arrived, several men in Company B received letters. Horace Alexander learned his wife died in January. He was heartbroken. He had worried about her the entire trip. He had such a hard time leaving her. The letter didn't say if the baby lived or not, or if he had a son or daughter." (Ricketts, 138)

With her dying breath, Nancy elicited a promise from Catherine that the three young daughters would be taken to the Salt Lake Valley to be with their father. Catherine kept her promise to care for the girls and brought them safely to Utah. In the spring of 1848, Horace was finally reunited with Frances Evelyn, Sarah Melinda, and Dionitia Emily;

eventually he married Catherine, the surrogate mother who had devot-
edly cared for his daughters and who had attentively nursed Nancy until
her spirit was released from a rasping, shivering frame (see Maynes, 25).

* * *

Precious in the sight of the Lord
is the death of His saints. —Ps. 116:15

Sparse Communication

COMMUNICATION, THE LIFEBLOOD OF FAMILY and community, was nearly nonexistent across the vast reaches of the continent during the early years of the Church. Just as persecution, disease, and harsh weather were obstacles of immense proportions for the Saints, so was the lack of communication a summit that could be surmounted only by sheer determination and unwavering faith.

The Mormon Battalion soldiers were the "trailblazers" to Santa Fe. Because the blazing of the trail was strenuous and treacherous, letters between soldiers and families were slow in transit, and it was not uncommon for soldiers who marched with the battalion to not receive any news about their families in Iowa throughout the entire duration of the march. Most were not aware of what was happening to the loved ones they had left behind.

The battalion soldiers left Iowa in July 1846 and arrived in California one year later, July 1847; at that time, most were discharged from service and continued walking on to Utah, arriving in the Salt Lake Valley in October 1847. But because few had received communication from their families, most of the men did not know whether their families had undertaken the trek west. In fact, the majority of the wives and children had not yet arrived in the Salt Lake Valley.

Most Battalion men, finding that their families were still in Iowa, straightway began walking back toward Winter Quarters and Council Bluffs—completing a round-trip journey of close to six thousand miles on foot. Most of these Battalion soldiers arrived in Iowa in December 1847.

Some had joyous reunions, returning to toddlers and not having known whether they would greet sons or daughters. But for others, the end of the journey brought unspeakable sorrow. Some walked all the way back to Iowa only to find that their beloved wives and children were no longer living. Joseph Shipley, husband of Elizabeth Garley Shipley, returned to Mount Pisgah searching for Elizabeth and their two sons. When he arrived, he was told that his wife and their youngest son, Nephi, had died of cholera. No one knew what happened to his other son, John. Joseph never saw any of his family again (see Maynes, 415).

Clarinda Bartholomew McCullough

Oh, if you were here I think I could talk all night . . .

CLARINDA ATLANTA BARTHOLOMEW AND Levi Hamilton McCullough were married in 1834 by Priest Tompkins of the First Congregational Church in Evans, Erie County, New York. When missionaries from The Church of Jesus Christ of Latter-day Saints arrived in Dryden, New York, where the young couple was living, both Levi and Clarinda listened to the messages preached by the newcomers, and in 1845 they were converted to this new "unpopular religion" (Maynes, 333).

When Levi was baptized, his father disinherited him. As specified in the will, Levi's inheritance was one dollar; Levi never saw his father's family again (see Maynes, 333).

After a brief residence in Michigan, the McCullough family settled in Nauvoo, where they watched the city transform from a sticky swampland into a bustling metropolis. Regrettably, they also watched as the shadows of persecution began to eclipse the hope of a peaceful community, and they were with the Saints who took flight across the Mississippi in February 1846. Just as they settled near Winter Quarters, Levi enlisted in the Mormon Battalion.

Clarinda was left in a covered wagon with her four small children. From her humble quarters, she wrote this letter to Levi:

> Dear Companion,
> The Lord has spared our lives although my trials are great and it seems sometimes as though I cannot live. The babe has not been well since you left us. . . . Henry has been

sick for about six weeks, but we are all getting better . . .
(Maynes, 334)

According to Clarinda, there had already been five deaths in the
camp since they had arrived.

A friend named Willis took up the call to help the McCullough
family, but he also became ill. Despite his weakened physical condition, Willis built a crude cabin for the family and did what he could to
provide food and sustenance for them. Clarinda pleaded for her husband's return in a report that described the desperate straits in which
the family existed:

> It is cold and your help is very much needed. I think that
> duty calls for you here if you are in the land of the living.
> Golden [the ox] is gone and I know not but he is dead.
> The cow gives about three pints of milk a day. I have had
> two pounds of sugar since you left me. You can judge that
> our living must be rather dry for "sis" wants the most of
> the milk. There is game here but I need someone to kill it.
> Willis has killed his white steer and he says that he shall kill
> Golden if he can find him. Willis is some better, but he does
> not know what to do for help. (Maynes, 334)

The battalion men sent money for provisions, but it was often
delayed:

> I do not get what you have sent short of giving half. I do not
> feel to find any fault with any of them, but I can tell you that
> it is a hard way to live. . . .
> We all want to see you very much. I have once more got
> my little children in a bed in a house. Thank the Lord, but I
> can scarcely see my line. Oh, if you were here I think I could
> talk all night. (Maynes, 335)

When Church leaders announced that the wagons would prepare
to move west, Clarinda expressed her doubt about her ability to follow
the counsel and again pleaded for her husband's return:

> We do not think that we can go unless we can have some-
> body to drive our teams. Do come and go with us and take
> care of the poor cattle. (Maynes, 335)

Clarinda ended her letter with a line that is, in retrospect, foreboding:

> I must bid you goodbye my dear husband, Levi H. Mc-
> Cullough. (Maynes, 335)

Clarinda died of consumption July 12, 1847, four days before Levi was released from service. Little Emily, age two, died three weeks later.

Unaware that his wife and daughter had departed this life, Levi returned to the Salt Lake Valley with the rest of the discharged soldiers and then completed the remainder of the journey to Iowa. When Levi arrived in Winter Quarters in December 1847, just a few days before Christmas, a friend gave him the sad news that Clarinda and Emily had died five months earlier. He found his remaining three children in various homes of family friends.

At one home, his son and daughter were brought into the room where Levi and two other men stood waiting. In testimony to the struggle through which Levi had survived, his son Henry asked his sister, Julia, "Which one of these ragged men is my father?" (Maynes, 335).

Levi reunited his surviving children and traveled west, arriving in the Salt Lake Valley in 1848. He never remarried, dedicating his life to being both father and mother to his children.

THE HOWLING PRAIRIE

A PICTURE OF THE DESTITUTE living conditions of the women who were left behind in Iowa can be gleaned from their earnest pleas for help as documented in their letters. One, Mary Hedrick Garner, wrote that she felt that her "experience at Council Bluffs was the hardest trial she ever passed through; harder than all the persecutions and sufferings in Nauvoo; she thought her heart would break" (Maynes, 217).

Maureen Ursenbeck Beecher, historian, wrote of Winter Quarters:

> Winter Quarters is not just a place. Winter Quarters is a time, a transition, and a trial. It is a cauldron, a crucible in which a people, converted to a new and demanding faith, were cleansed by cold and hunger, and baptized in a great pool of their suffering and redeemed by the outpouring of spiritual manifestation.

One description of the suffering of the "cauldron" and "crucible" is found in the words of of Brigham Young's nephew, John Ray Young, who was a child of ten at Winter Quarters. Later he wrote:

> Our house was near to the burying ground, and I can recall the small, mournful trains that so often passed our door. I remember how poor and shameful our habitual diet was and the scurvy was making such inroads among us that it looked as if all might be sleeping on the hill before spring. (Maynes, 141)

At times it must have seemed there would be no end to the misery. Numerous women, such as Mary Elizabeth Creager Shupe and Sarah Stuart Howell, lived in covered wagons for a full year (see Maynes, 267, 419).

Children were also pressed into sacrifice as they did whatever they could to help the family eke out survival. In order to support her family while her husband was gone, Louisa Maria Rose Sprague hired out by the week. Her five children were left to care for themselves. With no one else to get the wood, ten-year-old Eliza Ann went into the woods in deep snow and cut and dragged in wood to burn, making the trek shod in rags with her feet bound in fabric scraps (see Maynes, 444).

Countless other children were forced to care for their mothers and families, many without complaint despite the intolerable conditions. Seventeen-year-old Minerva Wade tells about caring for her mother, Sally Maria Bundy Wade, after both father and brother left with the battalion. Hoping to spare Minerva and her mother the stress of managing property, her father left his goods in the hands of a "friend," who straightway absconded with all their money and assets. Minerva wrote: "My pen fails to write of the sufferings, the ice and snow, the rain, the scanty provisions, the hard work but I do not remember any complaints of poverty or hardship. We were all working to go westward to our destination" (Maynes, 504).

Despite Minerva's affectionate care, her mother died of scurvy on October 13, 1848. So many Saints were sick and dying at that time that Minerva had to prepare her mother's body for burial. Rescue came in the form of William Hickman, who had come from Salt Lake to aid the Saints; he helped Minerva dig the grave and assisted her in burying her mother.

Soon after, William left for Salt Lake to help escort a company of Saints—but he returned to Iowa. He found Minerva and escorted her to the Salt Lake Valley, where they were married on May 1, 1849 (see Maynes, 504).

As the Saints arose from the "crucible of conversion," their spirits were sculpted and molded into new contours of faith: "O Lord, thou art our Father; we are the clay, and thou our potter; and we all are the work of thy hand" (Isa. 64:8). If the suffering on the howling prairie was unfathomable, then so was the love and artistry of the Savior.

Wolves

In the poems and writings of the Saints, wolves are a recurring theme and seem to be a metaphor for the anguish of loss the Saints encountered. Both men and women were influenced by the brooding howls of the wolves, and these words written by battalion soldier Levi W. Hancock seem to reflect not only the feelings of the Saints on the military march but also of those struggling for subsistence on the lonely plains.

Death of the Wolves

In memory of Elisha Smith

The battalion encamped
By the side of a grove,
Where the pure waters flowed
From the mountains above,
Our brave hunters came in
From the chase of wild bulls—
All around 'rose the din
Of the howling of wolves.

When the guards were all placed
On their outposts around,
The low hills and broad wastes
Were alive with the sound,

Though the cold wind blew high
Down the huge mountain shelves,
All was rife with the cry
Of the ravenous wolves.

Thus we watched the last breath
Of the teamster, who lay
In the cold grasp of death,
As his life wore away.
In deep anguish he moaned
As if mocking his pain,
When the dying man groaned
The wolves howled a refrain.

For it seemed the wolves knew
There was death in our camp,
And their tones louder grew,
And more hurried their tramp,
While the dead lay within,
With our grief to the full,
O, how horrid a din
Was the howl of the wolves!

Then we dug a deep grave,
And we buried him there—
All alone by the grove—
Not a stone to tell where!
But we piled bush and wood
And burnt it over his grave,
For a cheat, to delude
Both the savage and the wolf.

'Twas a sad doleful night!
We by sunrise, next day,
When the drums and the fifes
Had performed *reveille*—

When the teams were brought nigh,
And our baggage arranged,
One and all, bid *Good-bye*,
    To the grave and the wolves. (Ricketts, 312–313)

Mary Ann Hedrick Jameson

Pray for us. The weather is cold . . .

ON APRIL 6, 1834, FOUR years to the day after the Church was organized, Mary Ann Hedrick Jameson and her husband, Charles Jameson, were baptized. When persecution forced the Jameson family to
leave Ohio, they settled in Missouri. In October 1838, Mary Ann and
Charles lived with a group of Saints in a beautiful green area on the
banks of Shoal Creek in Caldwell County that came to be known as
Haun's Mill:

> Charles was one of those at Haun's Mill the day the mobbers
> came . . . and killed many boys and men. Charles was able to
> hide in a cornfield, but before he did he was wounded four
> times: twice in the stomach, once in the shoulder and once
> on the left side of his head. [The bullet tore away] a piece
> of the scalp exposing his brain. He . . . managed to crawl in
> a bush. The men followed him. One said "Shoot him." An-
> other said: "No let him suffer, he's dying anyway." However,
> he did not die. Mary nursed her wounded husband back to
> health. . . . These trials took a toll on Mary, as she lost twin
> babies at the time. (Maynes, 295)

After moving to Nauvoo, the Jameson family fled with the Saints
to the prairie of Iowa. They reached Mount Pisgah, intending to rest
there before continuing on to Council Bluffs, but their plans changed
abruptly when Charles enlisted in the battalion. It was a decision that

involved the entire family, since their oldest daughter—also named Mary—joined the battalion along with her husband, James B. Hiron. Mary stayed behind with her six other children, three of whom were married and her youngest, who was only two years old.

While Charles was away, Mary wrote this letter:

> To Charles Jameson—Mormon Battalion
> Dear Affectionate Husband:
>   I take up my pen to inform you that we are all in good health and I hope these few lines will find you well. The time is long to me since I seen you. I received but one letter from you since you left. I want to start in the spring to meet you somewhere. I see hard times but we hope for the better. Pray for us. The weather is cold, snowy, and stormy. I can't write anymore but remember your affectionate companion.
>   —Mary Jameson (Maynes, 296)

In December 1847, Charles returned to Iowa and was reunited with Mary and their children. The Jameson family remained in Iowa for two more years while they made preparations for their journey to the Salt Lake Valley; early in 1850, the arrangements were at last finalized. Only one obligation remained—they needed to sell their property, and Charles stayed behind to complete the transaction. All seemed to be falling perfectly into place. After surviving the battalion march and returning to find his family healthy and safe, Charles assumed that all was well. Then, shortly after Mary and the children departed, he received a letter:

> Indian Territory June 1850
> Dear Brother Jameson:
>   I wish to drop a line to you that perhaps may not be pleasant but never-the-less it is the truth. Mary, your wife, was taken with Cholera night before last about eleven o'clock and died before nine yesterday. We buried her in the best possible manner for the circumstances. The children are yet with us and doing well. We have buried five since yesterday morning: Shipley Redfield's child, Charlotte Thornton and Willis Johnson, the Bishop's son.

When you come out you will find the graves close to the road on the right hand, some eight or ten miles this side Salt Creek about ten miles from Kanesville. The whole camp had good health until the evening we crossed Salt Creek. There seems to be new fatal cases at present in the camp.

Alex [Charles's son] says that he does not know now if he can come back or not but wishes you to come out this season, if you can. If not, come in the spring early and he will meet you, if possible.

—Yours with respect,
Elisha (Maynes, 297)

Mary's son Hyrum, eight years old at the time, later told how his mother was wrapped in a white bedspread, the only funeral shroud that could be found for her burial.

Mary's children arrived safely in the Salt Lake Valley, where Charles later joined them. Charles Jameson carried the letter he received from Mary in his coat pocket throughout the rest of his life.

* * *

How firm a foundation, ye Saints of the Lord . . .

When through the deep waters I call thee to go,
The rivers of sorrow shall not thee o'erflow,
For I will be with thee, thy troubles to bless,
And sanctify to thee thy deepest distress.

When through fiery trials thy pathway shall lie,
My grace, all sufficient, shall be thy supply.
The flame shall not hurt thee; I only design
Thy dross to consume and thy gold to refine.

—Hymns, *85*

BLESSINGS

AFTER FIFTEEN YEARS OF DISRUPTION and unrest, possibly the greatest blessings these women and their husbands could have realized would have been peace, daily routine, health, shelter, and consistency. The Saints no doubt yearned for stability and certainty in their lives, for things reliable and persons dependable.

Ironically, they may have found their order and stability in the unfamiliar wilderness. On the placid stretches of prairie grass, a measure of daily organization and order began to appear, as reported in the observations of Colonel Thomas L. Kane:

> In the clear blue morning air, the smoke streamed up from more than a thousand cooking fires. Countless roads and by-paths checkered all manner of geometric figures on the hill sides. On the slopes, herd boys were seen lazily watching immense herds of cattle, sheep, horses, cows and oxen. Along the creeks . . . women, in great force would be washing and rinsing all manner of white muslins, red flannels, and particolored calicoes, and covering acres of grass-plat with their variously hued garments. Groups of merry children were playing among the tents. (Howe, 425)

Even though they were in transit, the pioneers enjoyed an interval of peace while building homes of a different kind in their own prairie world.

The interlude of peace was due to the fact that the camps were well organized and presided over by appointed leaders. The resulting community structure provided strength and refuge for Saints who had been too frequently and too abrasively torn from the moorings of previous security. Most importantly, the communal arrangement brought the Saints together, allowing them to love and serve each other, thus amplifying the power of charity. It has been said that the Lord has organized His Church so that His love could abound. While the Saints were not perfect, His love was perfect. And in the camps, love abounded.

Elizabeth Alden Pettegrew

The Lord thy God hath given his angels charge over thee;
thou shalt be preserved and not a hair of thy head shall fall
by the hand of an enemy.

WHEN ELIZABETH AND DAVID PETTEGREW were given a Book of Mormon, David said that "he knew it was not the words of the devil" (Maynes, 362). David was a prominent teacher at the Methodist Church in his Indiana neighborhood, and news that he had a copy of the Book of Mormon spread like wildfire. Those in his congregation feared he was "ruined" and that "his soul was lost forever" (Maynes, 363).

Undaunted by his congregation's denunciation, David invited his Mormon neighbor to speak at one of the weekly meetings held regularly in his home. At the meeting, the Mormon neighbor read from the twenty-ninth chapter of Isaiah and confidently proclaimed that "God brought this book forth by raising up a prophet and it was the fullness of the everlasting gospel."

As a result, the Pettegrew family was summarily excommunicated from the Methodist Church, and their serene country life in Indiana came to an end. Elizabeth and David set their course toward Missouri to be with the Saints, leaving their prosperous farm and large orchards behind.

David was industrious and resourceful, traits that were manifest many times during the journey to join the Saints. When the ship that was taking his family down the Ohio River ran aground and was stranded on a sandbar for five days, David purchased a small boat and continued down the river.

Later, when the family was on a steamer that ran into ice and stalled on the Missouri River, David quickly procured lodging for Elizabeth and the children, who were recovering from cholera. He continued on to Missouri alone, allowing his wife and children to rest while he appraised the farm area around Independence.

David selected an advantageous location for his farm, having chosen a plot of land situated on a well-traveled road leading to Fort Leavenworth, Kansas—a route that would eventually become a thoroughfare for the exchange of news and supplies. Here he built his home and settled his family.

Over time, the news and information obtained from travelers along that route began to concern David and Elizabeth; they were fearful and uncertain about the safety of their family. The winds of persecution had begun to blow upon them, battering their sense of well-being and security.

One night in particular, Elizabeth and David overheard a conversation concerning "how and what should be done regarding the Mormons in Missouri" (Maynes, 364). The conversation took on shadowy tones just as a looming storm outside their home exploded with thunder, lightning, and thrashing rains. In that night, storm foreshadowed storm.

Not long after, David was working in his field when he heard someone yelling that a mob was heading for his house. Frantic about his family's safety, he tore across the field back to his home, finding that Elizabeth and the children had already been driven into the street.

Desperate for any vestige of shelter, the family hid in a nearby cave; while they were temporarily safe from the mobs, they were not adequately protected from the elements. Chilled by the frigid winds that blew into the entrance of the cave, Elizabeth and five of her seven children again fell ill. After two days without food, and frozen by icy gusts of wind, the family was blessed by a man named Mr. Gates, who rescued them, befriended them, and supplied them with food and other provisions.

Over the next ten years, Elizabeth and David were forced out of three more homes. On one occasion they narrowly escaped violence by secretly slipping across the Mississippi River. In 1838, David fought in the Battle of Crooked River, where he was taken prisoner and confined to a filthy dungeon filled with spider webs and foul air.

During the culmination of the Missouri persecutions, Elizabeth and David were derided as being "British Tories." Because the Saints of that generation considered the American Revolution to be the touchstone of the American spirit and ideals, it must have been extremely painful to be called "British Tories." It was a wounding insult that implied ultimate betrayal.

Notwithstanding, or perhaps because of, their many years of suffering and problem solving, Elizabeth and David Pettegrew became spiritual stalwarts of the Mormon community. Constantly demonstrating unusual leadership abilities among the Saints, David and Elizabeth were well respected, and when the Mormon Battalion was being assembled, President Brigham Young personally asked David to enlist, explaining that he needed David "to act as a father figure and spiritual leader for the young men who were enlisting" (Maynes, 366).

David and Elizabeth were both fifty-four years old when President Young requested David's service in the battalion. Nevertheless, David followed the prophet's request, saying, "I then left my family in the care of my son in law . . . because I was counseled by President Young to go with the Mormon battalion, it being a particular request" (Ricketts, 17).

Elizabeth's twenty-one-year-old son, James Phineas Pettegrew, also enlisted in the battalion.

Seasoned figures of wisdom, strength, and sound judgment, David and Elizabeth now faced a chapter of separation in their lives. David received a letter of blessing from Patriarch John Smith, which read in part:

> Insomuch as you have left wife and children and all things that are near and dear to promote the interest of the Redeemer's kingdom here on earth, the Lord thy God hath given his angels charge over thee; thou shalt be preserved and not a hair of thy head shall fall by the hand of an enemy; thy life and health shall be preserved and [thou] shall return in peace to thy family. (Maynes, 366)

Patriarch Smith also promised that Elizabeth and the children would be protected and that David was not to be troubled about them. This was a cherished blessing for Elizabeth and David and their family.

Throughout the time of David's service with the battalion, the blessing given by the Patriarch was fulfilled. Five of Elizabeth's adult children were with her and able to care for her. She was further sustained as she extended her hand of charity and consolation to others in the encampment. She had gained many friends during the course of her life, and she garnered even more friends on the prairie as she served, drawing on the strength and wisdom acquired during a lifetime of trials.

When they eventually reached the Salt Lake Valley, Elizabeth and David continued to prosper. David became the bishop of the original Salt Lake Tenth Ward, and Elizabeth served at his side, continuing to bless the lives of those around them by virtue of the strength and knowledge acquired through the perils and tribulations they surmounted. Together they watched Salt Lake City expand and flourish.

BEAUTY IN THE
MAKESHIFT COMMUNITIES

AGAINST SCENES OF SUFFERING IN the crude encampments of Winter Quarters and Council Bluffs, the Saints made heroic efforts to beautify their surroundings and lift the spirits of the community. There were songfests, concerts, and dances; children were educated. Businesses, stores, trade, and industry appeared.

A new spirit of prairie gratitude germinated and grew in the hearts of many of the Saints, as is reflected in the words of Mary Haskin Parker Richards: "The place where we have settled for winter quarters is one of the most beautiful flats I have seen" (Maynes, 141).

Shirley Maynes, drawing on the history of Mary Jane Morris McCarty, wrote:

> When the Saints left their beautiful city of Nauvoo, they didn't realize that Iowa was an area known as a "beautiful land." Explorers and settlers of Iowa all agreed Iowa was so fertile and beautiful a land that one writer said, "it surpasses any portion of the United States." Isaac Galland, in the Iowa Emigrant (1840), described Iowa as a country of "surpassing fertility and beauty . . . One of the most sublime, terrestrial objects which the Creator ever presented to the view of man." . . . It seemed that the "Saints of God" were indeed in God's care. (Maynes, 330–331)

Enhancing natural prairie beauty, the Iowa landscape was further adorned with the prayers of the Saints, as described by Colonel Thomas L. Kane:

With the first shining of the stars, laughter and loud talking hushed, the neighbor went his way, you heard the last hymn sung and then the thousand-voiced murmur of prayer was heard like babbling water falling down the hills. (Howe, 428)

* * *

For the beauty of the earth,
For the beauty of the skies,
For the love which from our birth
Over and around us lies,
Lord of all, to thee we raise
This our hymn of grateful praise.

—Hymns, *92*

Pheby Jane Ferguson Cummings

Jane steeled her nerves and pulled out her husband's musket . . .

IN THE CONSIDERATION OF BLESSINGS, some of the most personal blessings received from the Lord are the deep intrinsic qualities and strengths, talents, and propensities that shape and mold a person's thoughts, views, abilities, and, ultimately, the events of life. Often the least recognized, these internal blessings of the spirit are the most significant. Pheby Jane Ferguson Cummings was blessed with a determined inner nature that belied the ordinary appearance of her life.

In natural possession of a strong will and independent nature, Pheby Jane Ferguson insisted at a young age that she be called by her middle name, Jane—a decision that was honored for the rest of her life.

Jane Ferguson married George Washington Cummings on July 5, 1833, in Michigan. As she began her life as a wife and mother, it was recognized that her spirited individualism often translated into a fierce determination to conquer any danger or opposition. This trait served her especially well as she faced the many challenges of the early days of the Church.

One such occasion occurred one evening while Jane lived in Hancock County, Missouri. She was home alone with her oldest son, Charles, who was ten at the time, when a belligerent mob approached her home at dusk. Menacing voices yelled for the two to leave, threatening to burn the house to the ground.

Taking a stand, Jane steeled her nerves and pulled out her husband's musket. She told the mob that they were welcome to try to burn the house down but that the first man who attempted to set fire would be shot dead. The mob backed down, and neither Jane nor Charles was harmed (see Maynes, 148).

Eventually, the Cummings's home and belongings were destroyed. Despite endless and earnest endeavors to defend their home and family, Jane and her husband, George, found themselves turning their backs and walking away from one farm after another. At length, when the time came to abandon Nauvoo, there actually might have been some comfort for Jane in the thought that each weary westward step put distance between her and the unruly mobs.

But as Jane and her family entered the vast wilderness of the prairie, the anticipated peace and well-being seemed once again beyond reach. As the early members of the Church gathered on the plains of Iowa and Nebraska, they would need to develop yet a greater physical and spiritual prowess in order to combat the new and harsh dangers that would threaten their very existence. A new assortment of adversaries awaited the Saints.

Grievous cold was the first remorseless enemy that battered the Saints. The frigid winter weather of Iowa and Nebraska was without sympathy, and numbing daytime temperatures ranged from thirty-four to twelve degrees Fahrenheit. The nighttime temperatures were exponentially colder, generally ten to thirty degrees below zero—much colder if the winds were blowing. Even more deathly were the punishing blizzards, raging with winds of up to sixty miles per hour.

Another callous enemy the Saints faced was disease. No one was safe from its snares; poor living conditions and malnutrition rendered many vulnerable. Men, women, and children fell victim, powerless to resist the various illnesses that swept through the camps.

When George picked up arms and marched away with the battalion, Jane made a home for herself and her four children in a wagon box. There they remained throughout the entire winter, susceptible to the ravages of both cold and disease. During the cold, blustery winds of winter, she and all four of her children contracted cholera—a virulent disease that caused severe dehydration and could kill within hours.

Tenacious, Jane survived. So did her ten-year-old son, Charles. But her other three children—seven-year-old Cornelius, three-year-old Harriet, and eight-month-old George—were unable to withstand the infectious epidemic that was augmented by the spiteful cold. While her husband marched through uncharted and unfriendly territory facing an uncertain war, Jane was faced with burying her three children.

When spring arrived, some of the Saints banded together to build a dugout for Jane and her son; even though it was a fairly primitive shelter, it provided greater protection than the wagon box.

Jane and Charles remained in the dugout until her husband, George, arrived back home. It was then that Jane learned that George had had the distinction of being a flag bearer for the battalion. In fact, it's believed that he designed the blue-and-yellow flag carried by the Mormon Battalion as its standard (see Maynes, 149).

Jane and George traveled west in 1852 and settled in Nephi, Utah. Even with her husband at her side, Jane continued to face demanding challenges. As one example, their first winter in Utah was so severe that their entire herd of livestock was lost to the freezing temperatures.

On another occasion during the 1853 Indian War, Jane and George were forced to move their rebuilt herd of livestock onto an island in the Great Salt Lake for protection. During that same year, George was called to ride Pony Express, where he weathered Indian attacks, bullet wounds, and the hot and cold seasons of the year.

During these challenges, Jane never failed to keep the hearth fires burning warm and secure.

On November 5, 1902, Jane Ferguson Cummings passed away. She was eighty-seven years old. Of the fourteen children that she mothered, only two survived to adulthood (see Maynes, 150).

Owing to her strong will and independent nature, Jane triumphed over the fury of mob persecution, the frozen grip of winter sheltered by nothing more than a covered wagon, a deadly disease, and the burying of twelve children. Her blessings were her will, her fortitude, and her faith.

MAKING HOME A BLESSING

THE TALENTS OF THE WOMEN in the early Church were many: mothering, listening, writing histories, sewing, creating needle arts, teaching music, organizing in many capacities, understanding unspoken thoughts and needs, keenly observing nature, practicing medicinal skills, and many others. But their greatest mission was to ensure the spirituality of the home. Regardless of how rugged and rustic that home may have been—sometimes nothing more than a wagon box—it was the mothers' concern that the "home" was a blessing for their families. Colonel Thomas L. Kane shared his perceptions:

> And they were a nation of wonderful managers. They could hardly be called housewives in etymological strictness, but it was plain that they had once been such, and most distinguished ones.
>
> Their art availed them in their changed affairs. With almost their entire culinary material limited to the milk of their cows, some store of meal or flour, and a very few condiments, they brought their thousand and one receipts [recipes] into play with a success that outdid for their families, the miracle of the Hebrew widow's cruse. . . .
>
> But the first duty of the Mormon women was, through all change of place and fortune, to keep alive the altar fire of home. Whatever their manifold labors for the day, it was their effort to complete them against the sacred hour of evening fall. (Howe, 427–428)

Mary Burrell Woolsey

Her name is written in the Lamb's Book of Life,
and shall be saved.

Blessings abounded among the early Saints who sacrificed so much for the gospel—and some of them came in the form of patriarchal blessings. Patriarch Hyrum Smith conferred upon Mary Burrell Woolsey a beautiful blessing, promising her that she "would be blessed with good health, an increase of prosperity and that her life would be preserved."

In addition, the blessing also promised that Mary "would receive an increase of blessings, henceforth, to comfort her heart with the spirit of God resting upon her." Finally, Mary was told, "Her name is written in the Lamb's Book of Life and shall be saved" (Maynes, 535).

Mary Burrell grew up a privileged daughter in an affluent plantation family in Cincinnati, Ohio. Her family eventually moved to Indiana, where she met and married Thomas Woolsey. She was sixteen years old on her wedding day, April 25, 1829, and one year later, their first child was born (see Maynes, 535).

After they had been married sixteen years, Mary and Thomas moved with their three children from Indiana to Brownstown, Illinois, where they were baptized members of The Church of Jesus Christ of Latter-day Saints. Enthused about their conversion, they joined the Saints in Nauvoo; were endowed on December 23, 1845; and were sealed on January 24, 1846. By then Mary and Thomas had five children.

When Nauvoo turned from a beautiful, peaceful city into one where the Saints lived in fear of animosity and attack, the Woolsey family saw that their only option for peace and well-being was to depart into the western wilderness. Fleeing in the winter exodus of February 1846, the family was threatened by temperatures that reportedly dropped below zero. Jessie Bennett, great-great-granddaughter, left this poetic description of the journey:

> For several days, river, earth and sky seemed frozen in a common immobility, varied only by the occasional gusts of wind that carried clouds of white through the thickets and groves, adding and taking away nothing of the whiteness that still wrapped them in what seemed an eternal blanket of numbing misery.
>
> During the second day, and for several days and nights after that, the white caravans of wagons and snow-beaten handcarts and miscellaneous carriages and even men and women on foot, carrying bundles, moved across the frozen river with only the rumble of the wheels and an occasional shout from the teamsters, to penetrate the glassy layer of cold and stillness that wrapped the earth. (Maynes, 532–533)

As Thomas brought his family to Mount Pisgah, he felt desperate for a source of income and enlisted in the Mormon Battalion. Knowing that his clothing allowance and wages would provide the necessary income for his family, he became a private in Company E. Before beginning the march, Thomas moved his family to Council Bluffs.

After Thomas's departure, Mary moved the family again, this time to Winter Quarters. During her stay in Winter Quarters, possibly the greatest blessing in Mary's life was the routine and repetition of organized activities. The children attended school, the families attended church, and the Saints socialized with those around them. Although illness ran rampant through the settlement during the winter months, Mary and her children remained healthy and in high spirits.

Thomas returned to his family a year later with a dramatic story to tell: After fulfilling his battalion service, and while he and his friend John Tippetts were returning to Winter Quarters on foot in the dead of winter, the two men were footsore, weather-worn, fatigued, and famished. Having exhausted their meager provisions, they were in a weakened state and unable to defend themselves when they were taken prisoner by Pawnee Indians. In the hands of an unfamiliar and unpredictable tribe, Thomas and John were condemned to death. Their situation seemed especially dangerous and inescapable when the tribe's chief unexpectedly arrived and, to the surprise of all, overturned their death sentence. The two brethren were set free, supplied with food, and sent on their way (see Maynes, 536).

Mary felt blessed. Her husband had returned safely. Her family was together, and each of her children was strong and healthy. Indeed, she was "blessed with good health, an increase of prosperity and that her [life was] preserved."

There was not much time for relaxation, however—shortly after Thomas returned to Winter Quarters, President Brigham Young asked him to move his family to Mount Pisgah, where he was assigned to grow produce to nourish the Saints who would be passing through the area on their way to Salt Lake.

The Woolseys served in Mount Pisgah until 1852, when they were finally able to travel west. They first settled in Weber Valley and then moved to Provo, where they remained until Mary died in 1858.

* * *

Let your hearts rejoice and be exceedingly glad. . . .
Let the earth break forth into singing. . . .
Let the mountains shout for joy, and all ye valleys cry aloud and
all ye seas and dry lands tell the wonders of your Eternal King!
And ye rivers, and brooks, and rills, flow down with gladness.
Let the woods and all the trees of the fields praise the Lord;
and ye solid rocks weep for joy! And let the sun, moon,
and the morning stars sing together, and let all the sons of God
shout for joy! And let the eternal creations declare his name forever
and ever! And again I say, how glorious is the voice we hear
from heaven, proclaiming in our ears, glory, and salvation, and honor,
and immortality, and eternal life; kingdoms, principalities, and powers!
—D&C 128:22–23

A Blessing of Peace

PEACE IS GENERALLY DEFINED AS a calm and quiet state free from tension, pressing concerns, and anxiety. It is often the quintessential promise and ultimate blessing of the Savior: "Peace I leave with you, my peace I give unto you, not as the world giveth, give I unto you. Let not your heart be troubled, neither let it be afraid" (John 14:27).

While in search of such peace, Eliza Collins Hunsaker's husband, Abraham Hunsaker, experienced a sweet miracle. While marching with the battalion, he had lain awake many nights worrying about his family. He continually pleaded with the Lord to protect his wife and children:

> One morning a dove flew into his camp and lit upon Abraham's shoulder. It stayed a moment then flew back over the trail they had just traveled on. Abraham watched the dove as far as he could see it. In his heart there was a feeling of peace. The next morning as he and his companions were preparing breakfast, the dove appeared again, circled around Abraham's head and flew away. He immediately realized that his prayers had been answered and he had the assurance that his loved ones were in God's keeping. (Maynes, 275)

* * *

The Lord will give strength unto His people;
the Lord will bless His people with peace.
—Ps. 29:11

 FRIENDSHIP

ELDER JEFFERY R. HOLLAND REMINDS us that "angels" often walk and talk with us in mortality in the form of the "angelic" people who surround us and serve us with love and devotion (see "The Ministry of Angels," *Ensign*, Nov. 2008). *Angelic* is the word that must also have come to the minds of the battalion women who were unselfishly served by their prairie sisters.

Witnessing hunger, they provided food. Sensing thirst, they gave drink. Seeing nakedness, they gave clothing. They took in strangers. To the sick they gave their time, sharing medical skills and optimism. They mourned with those who had cause to mourn. The women of the Mormon Battalion served each other and, in so doing, they served their Lord.

"In as much as ye have done it unto one of the least of these my brethren, ye have done it unto me" (Matt. 25:40).

As the sisters recognized the needs of others, angelic errands were performed, selfless service rendered, and forever friendships formed. Serving the Lord through service to each other, the women became friends—friends to each other and friends of Christ.

* * *

Henceforth I call you not servants . . . but I have called you friends.
—John 15:15

Mary Lee Bland Ewell
and Mammy Chloe

*I am sure I can never know what her great
devotion to me cost her . . .*

MARY LEE BLAND WAS BORN in 1817 to John and Sarah C. Lee Bland and grew up on the family plantation in what is now possibly southern Kentucky. Much of her upbringing was in the hands of her mother's personal slave, "Mammy Chloe," a beloved confidant and wise servant. Mammy Chloe's only family was a son named Sammy, about the same age as Mary Lee.

At a young age, Mary Lee was promised to Dale, the son of one of her father's friends. Because Dale's family's plantation neighbored the Blands's plantation, marriage between the two youth was desirable in maintaining family fortunes. Both fathers promised the couple a large parcel of adjoining land for a wedding gift. The engagement was to be announced when Dale came home from law school and Mary Lee from boarding school.

Mary Lee writes:

Dale and I broke up almost immediately after his arrival home because of ungentlemanly conduct. I tried to keep it from father as I felt he would not understand. Faithful old "Mammy Chloe" helped me to avoid Dale when he tried to see me again. Whenever he was seen coming I would slip out quickly and go for a ride on "Old Betsy."

One day no one was around to saddle her, so I did it myself. The cinche was not tight enough and while riding in the woods, some distance from home, the saddle turned, throwing me to the ground, injuring my back and my ankle.

As I lay there feeling unable to rise, a young man came along, bound my ankle and took me home. This young man introduced himself as William Fletcher Ewell, of Palmyra, Va., a medical student on vacation for the summer. During this vacation he was doing missionary work for the Church of Jesus Christ of Latter-day Saints, known as the "Mormons."

He was heartily welcomed and invited to make our home his own as long as he desired. This new religion was listened to and agreed with at first. Then one day father went to town and came back a changed man. He demanded an audience with William. My father had found in the community that the teachings of Joseph Smith and the Mormons were very unpopular. They had let father know that if he continued to entertain and encourage the young missionary that he would be an outcast. This was more than father could bear as his standing in the community was everything to him.

At first father tried to get William to give up teaching or believing this religion. When that was to no avail father commanded him in no uncertain terms to leave. When I pleaded both for the new religion and for William, I was ordered up to my room and forbidden to see William, or to leave the room until I changed my mind. My father locked the door. My mother was also forbidden to have contact with me until I changed my foolish ways.

I felt my heart would break for I loved William, and had a firm faith in the teaching which he had given us. I threatened to run away but Mammy Chloe said that would break my poor, ill mother's heart.

A week went by. Then came a message from William, by faithful Mammy Chloe. He wanted to know if I would be willing to go with him as his wife and be with the Saints.

My mind was made up. I knew the gospel was true and was worth any sacrifice; money and social position meant nothing to me in comparison to a life of usefulness with the one I loved. Mother was in sympathy and offered to help see that we could be together for she loved William as a son and wanted to see me marry for love rather than social position and to please parents as she had done.

It was decided that we would meet the next night before morning where William had found me that first day in the woods. Father in the meantime had offered me a trip to Paris hoping that would make me see things his way. I was not interested. Mama sent a purse full of money and a box of jewelry to me by Mammy Chloe as she was not permitted to come to me. Mammy also informed me that she had been given to me and that she would not think of letting me go without her to help me.

I made my escape through the second story window down the rose trellis. Sammy had two horses ready and waiting: one for Mammy Chloe and one for . . . me. I left a good-bye letter to mama with Zachary my brother, who was in sympathy with me.

We met William at the appointed place and rode all night in order to get far enough away that father would not follow. The next day we found a minister in a small town in Kentucky and we married with Mammy Chloe as my witness. I was not yet eighteen and William was just twenty. . . .

The following year our first son Francis was born while we were in Missouri with William's family during vacation. Mammy Chloe cared for him as she had cared for me when I was a baby. In due time another son John came to us and two years later a daughter, whom we named Sarah Elizabeth for dear Mama who still had not been permitted to see us.

The family [doctor] finally told papa that if he desired to keep his wife he had best let her see the daughter and grandchildren she had pined for so long in her weak condition.

Papa consented and we were sent for. We went promptly, even papa seemed happy to see us and loved the children. Our visit seemed to give new life to Mama.

Our happiness was complete until the day papa said, "Dr. Ewell, I want to have a talk with you. You seem to have made Mary Lee very happy and while I can't forgive you for taking her away as you did, I'll give you the strips of land we had planned to give Mary Lee and I'll build you a house as becomes our rank and you can practice medicine right here. You have made Mary Lee's mother happy and the Dr. says my wife hasn't long to live. But of course you will have to give up that abominable religion of yours for any social prestige among our kind."

William thanked him for his kind offer but said, "We cannot repudiate the truth of the gospel."

We were asked to leave and I was disinherited.

William had finished school that year. Mother soon passed away and my brother wrote that my portrait was thrown into the attic and my name taken from the family record in the Bible.

My jewels went one at a time in those times that followed. Another little girl, Barbara Ann, was born while we were living at Winter Quarters. Then came the call for volunteers to go to Mexico. William was among those who marched away on the longest military march in history, about two thousand miles. . . .

Three months after his goodbye our son William was born (MLB, 4–8).

In the meantime, William Fletcher Ewell wrote of his experiences with the Mormon Battlion. He recorded that he marched shoeless, his feet wrapped in rags. He fell ill but said he "could not give up." His most important aim was to reach his family in Iowa; he was determined to see his wife and four children.

Mary Lee continues her memoir, telling of William's return to Iowa:

His health seemed to improve some, he was home and we were happy, then privations in that terrible winter of 1847–48 caused a relapse and after a promise exacted from me that I would take the family and go with the saints to Zion, he passed from this life in my arms, leaving me grief stricken and facing maternity again with Mammy Chloe my only attendant.

Little Mary Jane was born four months after her father's death.

We then set about to keep our pledge that we go to Salt Lake, the Zion of the mountains. Oh how I missed William, always so faithful to the Church, so kind and true.

I could have gone back to luxury at home by repudiating our faith but was not tempted, even in the face of poverty.

So in about two years' time my faithful Mammy Chloe helped me bring my family to the Salt Lake Valley. We located in Cottonwood and Mammy taught me to spin and weave materials for our clothes, make carpets for the floor. She taught me how to card wool and to make quilts.

She also taught me how to weave straw hats like the ones the darkies made in the South. I managed to create a little fancy style and Mammy Chloe sold them to the stores and other settlers. Thus we made our living until my sons were old enough to earn and make a home for us.

Poor old Mammy Chloe loved the Gospel. I taught her to read, and she often remarked, "I'd be willin', honey, to be skinned alive if I could jus' go in dat temple."

Even after the slaves were freed by Pres. Lincoln she did not desire her freedom. No one ever knew her grief, leaving her own boy Sammy, but being slaves they learned never to complain at separations. I am sure I can never know what her great devotion to Miss Mary Lee, as she always called me, cost her and how she softened all my hardships wherever she could.

I never made an effort to recover my rights in my father's estate. However, I feel that I have been compensated by living in the shadow of God's Temple. . . .

I will never go back home now, but I hope that some of my posterity will go down South and rescue the portrait of little Mary Lee Bland (MLB, 10–12).

It is interesting to note that when Mary Lee escaped from home to marry William and be with the Saints, she received two gifts from her mother: a favorite slave and a collection of jewels. When a landed woman of the South married, she gave up all title to her land and any other wealth she may have acquired. She was allowed to keep only two things as her own: her slaves and her jewels. Apparently, the night that Mary Lee and Mammy Chloe rode away from the plantation on Old Betsy, Mrs. Bland had given all that she possessed to Mary Lee.

Certainly, one of the most endearing notes about this story is the devotion of Mammy Chloe to Mary Lee and the lifelong companionship that developed between the two women. Perhaps one of the most telling moments of sincere friendship in this story is when Mammy Chloe teaches Mary Lee to spin and card wool, and in return Mary Lee teaches Mammy Chloe to read and write. When reading the words of Mary Lee, one senses a deepened friendship forged through time, hardship, discovery, and reverence.

Mary Lee Bland Ewell died May 24, 1898, and is buried at San-taquin, Utah. Before her death, she completed temple ordinances for many of her family members. Perhaps sweetest of all, temple work was performed for Mammy Chloe and her son, Sammy, on November 10, 1987 (see Maynes, 192–193).

Becoming One

THE NATURE OF CHARITY THAT anchored the friendships of these pioneer women provided a supportive united sociable environment. Women in the pioneer community often "came together in neighborhood groups to gather food, to quilt, braid straw, comb each other's hair, knit, wash clothes, and read letters" (Maynes, 10). Within the community, this sisterhood was a link to health, to life, to hope, and to their Heavenly Father.

In the strain and exertion of living in a wilderness, compassion mothered ingenuity. It was through *service* that knowledge was acquired and shared. Service reinforced an iron-like bond between the sisters—a bond that was stable, reliable, and powerful in times fraught with instability, uncertainty, and powerlessness.

To read about the services rendered by these faithful women is to read about a wide variety of unique personal gifts—personal capacities and talents that were refined as if in a smelting procedure.

Beautiful metals emerge from the smelting process when heat and pressure are applied to raw ores that are melted and sometimes fused with other ores in order to separate, identify, purify, and render the different metallic components.

Just as precious metals become recognizable through the high temperatures of smelting, so did the exquisite and priceless talents and attributes of the Saints emerge into recognition during the heat and pressure of their fiery trials. And just as precious metals are recognizable as heated ores fuse together, so were the personal and spiritual gifts distinguished, purified, and rarefied as the people on the prairie fused together in helping and protecting one another.

As the people merged and melted together in the deepest ravines of affliction, sharing the most profound expressions of charity, personal identity and polished talents appeared in a refined and brilliant state.

The bright individuality of each sister was illuminated as she gave her will to the Savior for the welfare and unity of the entire community. In the process of becoming "one," individuality shimmered.

Medicinal Ministrations

ONE OF THE MOST REMARKABLE characteristics of the women on the prairies was their sympathetic and caring attitude as they nursed each other to health. Many friendships were strengthened through benevolent medicinal care. Colonel Thomas L. Kane expressed his admiration for the life-giving compassion of the women in Council Bluffs and Winter Quarters:

> Inside the camp, the chief labors were assigned to the women. . . . They were the chief comforters of the severest sufferings, the kind nurses who gave them in their sickness those dear attentions with which pauperism is hardly poor, and which the greatest wealth fails to buy. (Howe, 427)

The history of this period is replete with countless narratives of women ministering health and well-being one to another.

One of the most poignant moments of Sarah Beriah Fiske Allen's story occurred when she was so near death that those around her whispered messages for her to deliver to spirits on the other side of the veil. She was saved by an unnamed sister who refused to let her die. This "angel of mercy" held Sarah in comforting arms, spooned warm liquid down her throat, and helped her swallow until she could swallow by herself (SA, 3).

Young Amy Ann Marble Babcock, ill from scurvy, had been bedridden for two months when Fanny Parks Taggart came to care for her. Amy Ann's limbs were so drawn and her muscles so contracted that she could not stand on her feet, much less walk even a single step. A determined caretaker unwilling to accept Amy Ann's infirmity, Fanny combined vinegar and pepper and rubbed the mixture on Amy Ann's legs and feet. Fanny also procured some "relaxing oil" and a pair of crutches. Thanks to Fanny's tender care and loving shepherding, Amy Ann was soon able to move independently (see FPT, 2).

Other women were remembered for the specific skills and talents they so willingly shared with those around them. Sophronia Arminia Scott Standage was "a highly educated woman who taught children to read and write." She was also an expert in growing herbs and knew how to use them in food preparation and for health purposes (Maynes, 450).

Sarah Ann Arterbury Church, a midwife who was described as a large, good-natured, and hardworking woman, was also fondly remembered for her knowledge of medicinal herbs:

> Her skills and services in this critically needed specialty are mentioned many times in the early historical records. She knew how to use herbs and medicinal teas to aid in the care of the families. Among them were Yarrow, Tansy, Slippery Elm, Spearmint, Catnip and Peppermint. Sulfur and molasses were used for sore throats and warm olive oil was used for earache. Pine gum was the regular common medication for "drawing" infected places. Roasted onions and syrup made from onions and sugar was given for colds. (Maynes, 118, 119)

As these women of the prairie ministered to each other as doctors and nurses, they became each other's closet angel-sisters.

Elizabeth Harris Browett

Loss eased by friendship . . .

THE FOLLOWING PROSE, WRITTEN BY Roxanne Grey, is based on true incidents from Elizabeth Harris Browett's life.

> I am happy to hear that you have remained well. Be of good cheer, Elizabeth. It brings me happiness to know that you are continuing to pursue the course since hearing the glad sound of the gospel. I would also like to be called a worthy servant of God and hope I will be found worthy of God's graces and love.
> —Love, Daniel (Maynes, 64)

Elizabeth returned the letter to her apron pocket. She felt a warm smile spread across her face. Sitting on the porch, she listened to the children playing nearby. Squeals of laughter rose up from the tall grasses and trickled into the cool, evening air. Suddenly, there was a rustling, and the grasses parted to reveal an energetic jumble of arms and legs. The children leapt to their feet and ran screaming across the dirt road that ran in front of the house.

"Aunt Browett, Aunt Browett! Look!"

Elizabeth held out her arms as her nieces and nephew bounded toward her. The littlest girl jumped into her lap and pointed as the rest of the children began to cartwheel head over heels. Elizabeth laughed and clapped her hands, applauding the chaos. Some fell to their knees and, without pausing for breath, jumped back up and tried again. The littlest girl in Elizabeth's lap jumped down and began to laugh and cheer for each of her older brothers and sisters.

Just as they had tired of the tumble, their mother came around the corner of the house and the show began again. Elizabeth smiled as Hannah gathered the children into her arms.

"You must show your father!" she said. "Robert, come see what the children have mastered!"

Robert was Elizabeth's brother and Hannah her sister-in-law. The laughing rivalry reminded her of times when she herself had laughed and cheered for her older brother at his boxing matches in Gloucester County, England. It was at such a sports event that she met her husband, Daniel Browett. After they were married, Daniel and Elizabeth joined the Church alongside Robert and Hannah. All four made the trip across the ocean to Nauvoo.

Daniel and Robert left with the Mormon Battalion shortly thereafter. Elizabeth, who had no children of her own, helped to look after Hannah's six children that cold winter. The family made it to the Salt Lake Valley, and Robert soon returned to greet them. Elizabeth could remember how anxious she was the next few months awaiting her own husband's return.

But Daniel would not return.

In the spring of 1848, Daniel was chosen to be a part of a small group of men who traveled ahead to find a better trail through the Sierra Mountains. Their path of duty led them into peril. Captured, tortured, and finally murdered by Indians, Daniel and his companions were buried at Tragedy Springs.

Living in Salt Lake, Elizabeth remained a beloved member of her brother's family. Fortified by the memories that her husband's letters evoked and fueled by her knowledge of eternal families, Elizabeth continued to pursue the path that they had started together. She finished her course "a worthy servant of God."

FRIENDSHIP

How sweet is friendship's cheering voice,
When far from kindred parted;
It makes the lonely breast rejoice,
Or cheers the gloomy-hearted.
Although in distant lands we roam,
Disconsolate and weary,
From old companions and from home,
In regions lone and dreary.

Then Friendship's sweet angelic sound
Can cheer those scenes of sorrow,
And joys more pure in them are found
Than wealth can buy or borrow.
If from celestial realms of Bliss
This principle we sever,
No happiness could there exist,
No heaven there . . . no never.
—Sylvester Hulet
Mormon Battalion soldier (Ricketts, 309)

* * *

Cultivating Native American Friendships

Among the women left behind when their husbands marched away, there were those whose fulfillment and gift was to reach outside of their immediate circles.

Lucretia Charlotte Bracken Maxwell was one such woman. She was adept at building camaraderie with Indian women, spending many hours sharing with them her methods of sewing and cooking. At one point, she adopted a three-month-old Indian girl, whom she named Imogene (see Maynes, 328).

Another such woman was Clarinda Cutler Raymond, who also built a loving rapport with the Indians, most often by nursing their sick children to health. The depth of her Indian friendships was evident by the many who attended her funeral, "chanting mournful cries" (Maynes, 388).

Still another was Mary Napier Rowe, who had the gift of prophecy and of tongues. On one occasion, she taught an Indian, James Onumph, the gospel in his native language. Partly as a result of her patience and friendship, James soon became a member of the Church and later served in a bishopric (see Maynes, 396–397).

For the women of the prairie, compassion was at the base of friendships both inside and outside immediate circles. Love could, and did, cross social borders.

* * *

The rich have many friends. —Prov. 14:20

Jane Louisa Jones Canfield and Clarissa Lora Jones Canfield

Sisters can be the very best friends.

JANE LOUISA AND CLARISSA LORA were born to a prominent family in Richland, New York; parents Horace and Laura Jones were descended from stalwart early American forebears who held important governmental positions in the first colonies that settled America. In 1776, those ancestors had boldly taken arms against England.

Jane Louisa, who chose to be called Louisa, was three years older than Clarissa. Both were married to Cyrus Culver Canfield (see Winter Quarters).

While Cyrus was serving in the battalion, both women traveled west with the Heber C. Kimball Company—a company that was comprised of 662 Saints, 226 wagons, 96 pigs, 299 chickens, 17 cats, 52 dogs, three beehives with bees, three doves, five ducks, and one squirrel (see Maynes, 101).

The following prose, written by Roxanne Grey, is based on the incidents of Louisa's and Clarissa's lives:

The sun assertively made itself known. Clarissa wiped her forehead with the hem of her apron and smiled weakly at her sister. Louisa reached over and gave her hand a quick squeeze. It was only just after noon and the two women had already fallen behind the company. This seemed to happen almost every day. Each morning the two sisters rose before the rest of the camp to eat breakfast, and clean up. They did everything they could to prepare for the day's journey, but they did not have the strength to yoke their own team of oxen. Forced to wait, they watched anxiously until the men could help them.

In a wagon train of over six hundred saints, Clarissa and Louisa were determined to not fall behind. Every day they struggled to keep up with the other teams and every night they fell into a deep sleep, heavy with exhaustion.

Sometimes Clarissa found the energy to dream that the battalion would suddenly appear over the horizon, imagining her husband calling out to her. But today, even her imagination failed her. All of her strength was given to the enduring of the hot sun, and to the listening of the plodding of the oxen.

The two sisters were accustomed to being alone. They both joined the Church as young women, leaving their parents and home in New York to be with the Saints. It had been a sorrowful parting. Tightly they had grasped each other's hands as they left their home and began walking the roads westward. There was no doubt in their minds that they were going to the right place.

First Louisa and then Clarissa married Cyrus Canfield. Clarissa gave birth to a son, Myron. Louisa helped to care for her nephew even as the family was forced to leave Nauvoo. When Cyrus left with the battalion, Louisa helped Clarissa and Myron cross the Mississippi into Winter Quarters.

When young Myron died just one year later, Louisa helped her sister bury her baby boy.

Now, the days seemed to run together in quiet monotony. They knew that they were making progress, but they were tired, so very, very tired. Though they had no idea what was waiting for them in the West, once again they knew they were going to the right place.

Louisa began to hum softly under her breath. "Be still, my soul . . ."

A sudden breeze bent the tall grasses, tossing Clarissa's hair. The air cooled the sweat on her face, and she smiled contentedly. "The Lord is on thy side . . ." (see D&C: 84:99–102).

ROMANCE

YOUNG LOVE BABBLES LIKE A mountain stream; mature love, like a wide river, possesses power. Over time and distance, young streams develop into wide rivers; time and distance can also change love, giving power to its passion. And, just as rain fills the streams that become rivers, romance deepens and strengthens the love that can move mountains.

Romance for the men and women of the battalion was atypical. Cow chips rather than candles lit their dinners. Flowers, if there were any, were not hothouse but "hot prairie" grown. Though atypical, however, their romances were real. Husbands and wives cherished each other and showed their devotion in both word and deed, finding ways to be together when it was all but impossible and writing letters when being together was truly impossible.

Fostered by romance, their love became powerful—more powerful than the mobs that tried to destroy them; more powerful than the miles that stretched between them; more powerful than the disease, hunger, and heartache than plagued them; more powerful even than the death that eventually separated them.

If their love was powerful on earth, it will be even more powerful in heaven. They were parted at death, but they will unite again in eternal life. And, reunited, they will share in a fullness of glory forever.

* * *

And again, verily I say into you, if a man marry a wife
by my word, which is my law, and by the new and everlasting
covenant . . . it shall be said into them—

Ye shall come forth in the first resurrection;
and if it be after the first resurrection, in the next resurrection;
and shall inherit thrones, kingdoms, principalities, and powers,
dominions, all heights and depths . . .
and they shall pass by the angels, and the gods,
which are set there, to their exaltation and glory in all things,
as hath been sealed upon their heads,
which glory shall be a fullness and a continuation of the seeds
forever and ever. —D&C 132:19

Polly Matilda Merrill Colton

A BEAUTIFUL BRUNETTE WITH LARGE brown eyes, Polly Matilda Merrill was considered the prettiest girl in town. In the small community of Shelby, Michigan, she was frequently the center of attention as the young men flocked around her as often as parents or work would permit. Rather small in stature and very demure, she caught the interest of a young Mr. Philander Colton.

It was common talk among the boys of the village that no boy could kiss Polly Merrill. Accepting the challenge without apology or trepidation, Philander proudly boasted about his prowess and immediately sought opportunity to accomplish the mischievous deed. One evening at a country party, a group of girls was seated on some benches in the shade of a stand of trees. Philander recognized his opportunity and, slipping up behind, he grabbed shy Polly by the shoulders and planted a succulent kiss on her cheek. Angrily, she slapped him in the face (see Maynes, 133).

Philander was unrepentant. He bragged, "I told the fellows I would, and I shall do it many other times in the future" (Maynes, 133).

Philander made good his promise. Despite her indignant reception of his arrogant introduction, Polly married Philander on July 3, 1833.

Several years later, Parley P. Pratt arrived as a missionary in Michigan and taught the gospel to Polly and Philander. In 1839, Philander joined the Church, and a year later Polly was baptized.

Polly and Philander eventually arrived in Council Bluffs, where Philander enlisted as private in Company B of the Mormon Battalion. As Philander marched southward toward Fort Leavenworth, Polly's oldest son, twelve-year-old Charles Edwin, stole away from his mother's watchful eye and joined his father in the battalion march. A persistent young Charles stayed with the battalion, eventually becoming an officer's aide.

Both father and son remained with the battalion, marching all the way to California. When they were released from duty, they left for Salt Lake, where Philander left Charles with a great-uncle while he returned to Iowa to find his wife. Charles arrived in Iowa at Christmas time, making the holiday an especially precious occasion for him and his family.

The Colton family journeyed to the Salt Lake Valley, where they spent many happy years together. Philander worked as a brick mason and plasterer, and Polly cared for their household of eleven children.

On August 13, 1891, at the age of seventy-three, Polly passed away, but even her passing was marked by romance. While she was bedridden, the family told Philander that she was dying. He responded firmly, "No, she won't leave me. When we were married she promised to stay with me and she has never broken a promise yet." After Polly's death, Philander instructed his family, "Don't bury her until I die. When you hear a loud clap of thunder, I'll pass away also." Only two days later—on August 15, in the midst of a cloudless sky—a loud clap of thunder sounded. Philander closed his eyes in death at that very moment (Maynes 135–136). United in life, they were united in death.

Both Polly and Philander Colton were buried in the Maesar Cemetery near Vernal, Utah.

On My Word

If I say
I'll wait for you
at a certain place,

I will stay
until moss creeps
over my north side,

swallows mud a nest
in my hair, return,
year after year,

wind tatters and flaps
my clothes
alarming crows,

and roots grow down
from my heels
and each toe

should you ask
me to wait.

—Helen Beaman, 2008 (Beaman, 7)

Fanny Parks Taggart

To hide my tears I turned quickly away and said nothing.
Well, thought I, this will never do, I must do something . . .

IN HER PATRIARCHAL BLESSING, FANNY Parks received divine and noble promises:

> Thou shalt be numbered among the virtuous and thy mind stored with understanding, and in the due time of the Lord thou shalt have a companion. He shall be a mighty man of God and thou shalt raise up posterity endowed with the holy Priesthood that shall go forth to carry the gospel to nations yet unborn. (Taggart, Fany Parks [FPT], 4)

At the age of twenty-four, Fanny met her promised companion— George Washington Taggart, who truly was a "mighty man of God." George Taggart had been married previously, but his wife had died, leaving him with a two-year-old daughter named Eliza Ann. A carpenter with beautiful dark hair and penetrating blue eyes, George became Fanny's husband on July 12, 1845 (Taggart, George Washington [GWT], 2). Fanny adopted Eliza Ann heart and soul and, considering her as her own daughter, she wrote, "Through all the hardships and trials to come I had her with me . . . she was a great comfort to me" (FPT, 1).

Fanny and George received their endowments on January 12, 1846, and were sealed for time and all eternity.

Only seven months after they were sealed, George left to serve as an artillery guard in the first company of Saints leaving Nauvoo. Fanny remained behind with Eliza Ann, intent on selling their property to earn some income for the journey to Winter Quarters. She wrote,

> When my husband left me in Nauvoo I was sick with the chills and fever, but as the weather got warmer I got better and my health was good for most of the time while he was gone which I considered a great blessing. (FPT, 1)

Unfortunately, George and Fanny's land did not sell, but Fanny made the decision to join her husband nonetheless, hoping that her circumstances would improve once she reached Iowa and was reunited with George. But George was not in Iowa when Fanny arrived. He had already left with the battalion, and two years would pass before she would see him again.

While temporarily waiting at Mount Pisgah, George had heard that Brigham Young was asking for volunteers to serve in a Battalion. He enlisted as fifer in Company B, playing a fife that he carved himself (GWT, 9). On July 8, 1846, the day before he left Mount Pisgah for Council Bluffs, George had written to Fanny telling her of his decision to enlist with the battalion:

> Beloved and respected Wife, it is with grief and disappoint-ment, although mingled with bright prospects of the future that I sit down to pen a few lines to you concerning the sudden change that is about to come across my calculations. I expect the disappointment will be as great to you as to Myself. I had calculated from the time that I stopped at this place until this morning that I should see you and Eliza Ann before I left. . . .
>
> My faith is that you will not murmur at my volunteer-ing to absent myself from you for so long inasmuch as I go by council of the church.
>
> You may be assured Fanny it is a great disappointment and a wound to My natural feelings to tear Myself as it were away from My Family that I have not seen for five months, and when I have been imagining to Myself for the last week that you were almost in sight. But I believe that the God of Israel will order all things right for those that act through a

pure desire for the welfare of his Kingdom, this is the motive through which I hope always to act. . . .

Take good care of Eliza Ann and tell Her that Her Father is sorry to go away and not see Her and Mother, but tell Her to be a good girl and not forget her Father. . . . May the Lord bless you with life and health and with every necessary blessing and keep you steadfast in the principles of truth and virtue until We meet again, this is and shall be the prayer of your absent but affectionate Companion. (GWT, 9)

Fanny wrote in her autobiography her feelings upon hearing of George's enlistment: "It seemed awfully hard to me. I had no one to look to and not a penny of my own . . . so it looked very discouraging" (FPT, 1).

On August 6, 1846, George wrote another letter to Fanny:

Beloved companion,

I now improve an opportunity which presents itself in writing a few lines to you thinking that it will be some consolation to you to know that I am yet alive and have not forgotten My Wife. I am in good health, and you may well suppose that I am anxious to hear from you as I have not heard from you since your letter of the second of June. I feel a great anxiety to hear from you for I fear that you must have been in want of provisions. . . . I feel concerned for fear I have left you to suffer. . . .

I feel Fanny as though I had made as great a sacrifice as I could well make, in that I have forsaken for the time being My possessions, My Family, and at the risk of life start for Mexico as a united States Soldier with 500 of My Brethren in order to show that the Blood of my Grandfathers who fought and bled in the revolutionary war and the spirit of liberty and freedom still courses in the veins of some of their posterity that are called Mormons.

I go forward on this expedition with full faith and confidence that I shall have your prayers and blessings and that My life will be preserved and that I shall again have a joyful meeting with you and Eliza Ann and enjoy a long and happy life here upon the Earth. (GWT, 9–10)

Trials challenged but failed to conquer Fanny's positive outlook. She wrote:

> When I arrived at Winter Quarters I was looking for the families of the battalion to be assisted, but everyone had to do the best they could and as I had no relatives there, I did not know how to act nor what to do.
>
> So I went to President Brigham Young and asked him what I had better do and he told me to hunt up some acquaintances and get in with them until I could get myself a house.
>
> On my hearing this the tears came to my eyes and I felt like having a good cry, and to hide my tears I turned quickly away and said nothing. Well, thought I, this will never do, I must do something, then wiping my eyes looked up and saw a tent and in the door stood one of the sisters. I went to her and inquired if she could tell me where Father Asa David lived.
>
> She showed me his house and I went there and was made welcome to such accommodations as they had. Their house was a small log one with no floor nor window, but a piece had been sawed out of one of the logs for the light to enter. When it was not too cold I slept in their wagon. (FPT, 2)

Fanny continued to move from one family to another, providing service and accepting whatever accommodation could be offered her. While living with Amy Ann Babcock, she was given a room in which to live but she had to procure her own food. Commenting on her bill of fare, she wrote that her meals "consisted mostly of corn boiled in weak lye water to take off the husks, then washed and boiled until tender. I can remember of thinking it quite a treat when a child, but come to live on it for months it was quite another thing" (FPT, 2)

George knew nothing of Fanny's circumstances, and he began to pen another letter on September 19, 1846:

> I am yet in tolerable health. Brother Pace, Lee & Egan came up to the battalion . . . with letters from the Mormon Camp, and you may expect that I was greatly disappointed when I

learned that there was no letter for me, neither did I learn any verbal information concerning you. . . . but wherever you may be I hope this will find you and Eliza Ann enjoying the blessing of life and health. (GWT, 11)

When George reached Santa Fe in October, he was finally able to send the letter he had been carrying for a month, to which he added:

> I have carried this letter which I supposed I had finished at the time I wrote it. . . .
> Fanny I feel anxious to hear from you & My Little Daughter and I am more anxious to see you, but distance and circumstances forbids Me the latter privilege. But I trust that Our minds and feelings are not separated although distance between us may intervene. (GWT, 12)

He wrote that he planned to include some money in the letter, and explained,

> I send for your benefit at this time 19 dollars and 4 cents. . . . I wish I could send you a thousand dollars but that you know is out of the question. . . . My health is good and I am blessed, and I do not forget to remember you in My prayers to the Lord, be faithful and true and again I'll meet you. (GWT, 12)

Letters such as this one were Fanny's sole comfort as she struggled on her own, moving from family to family and working for whatever compensation could be offered her.

George marched all the way to California with the battalion, then returned for Fanny, who was living with Mrs. Charles Lambert at the time. Of the meeting, Fanny wrote, "The little girl, Eliza, had forgotten her father" (FPT, 3). It had been a long separation; they had been apart for twenty-two months.

While the separation had been long, the reunion was correspondingly sweet. Affectionate arms replaced perishable pen and paper. Fanny was thankful to have her husband at her side.

Fanny wrote a poem reflective of her devotion:

> Ever may your path be peaceful
> Duty is the road to fame
> Great and glorious things await you
> As you strive a crown to gain
> Right and truth be ere your motto
> May you true and faithful be
> On your God rely in trouble
> Never fail to bow the knee.
> Truth and right will always conquer
> Of your Father now take care
> Ever listen to His council
> Love and cherish Him while here. (FPT, 4)

The last words in Fanny's autobiography testify of the Prophet Joseph Smith:

> I often think of the many happy hours listening to the words of life that flowed from the lips of the Prophet. No one could help but like him for he was kind and good. I have heard him reprove men for their wrong doings and talk pretty sharp but it was always in such a good spirit that it appeared to me that no one could be offended. I have heard him talk a great many times and can bear testimony that I always felt benefited and I know he was a prophet of God and that the Lord called him in His own due time to lay the foundations of His latter day work. (FPT, 4)

* * *

The Lord hath brought again Zion;
The Lord hath redeemed His people, Israel,
According to the election of grace,
Which was brought to pass by the faith
And covenant of their fathers.
The Lord hath redeemed His people;
And Satan is bound and time is no longer.
The Lord hath gathered all things in one.
The Lord hath brought down Zion from above.
The Lord hath brought up Zion from beneath.
The earth hath travailed and brought forth her strength;
And truth is established in her bowels;
And the heavens have smiled upon her;
And she is clothed with the glory of her God;
For He stands in the midst of his people.
Glory, and honor, and power, and might,
Be ascribed to our God; for He is full of mercy,
Justice, grace and truth, and peace,
Forever and ever,
Amen.
—*D&C 84:99–102*

Matters of the Heart

ABIGAIL HAWS TUTTLE

The morning the battalion marched away, Abigail Haws waved a fond farewell to her most beloved friend, Luther Tuttle. That evening, after putting in a long day and feeling emotionally depleted, she was on her way to a meeting with some friends when a small boy ran after her saying that there were some men who wanted supper. She replied curtly, "We don't care to get supper for tramps." But for reasons unknown, she and her friends decided to prepare a meal for the men after all.

When the "tramps" entered the dining area, there stood Luther with two of his friends from the battalion; the three young men had returned to Winter Quarters to see their sweethearts!

Early the next morning, Elder George A. Smith performed a ceremony that united Abigail Haws and Luther Terry Tuttle in marriage. Abigail, now a married woman, watched her husband, Luther, march away—for the second time—as he hurried to catch up with the battalion (see Maynes, 492).

ANN FARAGHER KELLY

Ann Faragher Kelly was born in Marown, Isle of Man, England, and immigrated to America. A gentleman named William Kelly, who had been born in the same town in England, also immigrated to America. The two were married July 19, 1846—the evening before the battalion departed.

No one knows whether Ann and William were acquainted with each other before leaving England, but whatever the extent of their prior friendship, the depth of their love was recognized and solemnized the night before the battalion marched away (see Maynes, 313).

CYRENA DUSTIN MERRILL

In early 1804, Cyrena Dustin met Philemon Merrill at the home of Stephen Markham, where she was employed, and her presence in the home prompted a fascinating prediction:

> In February 1840, Philemon was passing through Nauvoo from Fort Madison to Carthage, when he stopped by to see his old friend, Stephan Markham, who invited him for dinner. [Cyrena] waited on the dinner table, and after dinner was finished, Philemon asked his friend who the young lady was. When his friend told him, Philemon remarked: "I'll be back here some day for she will be my wife." (Maynes, 337)

Philemon's statement proved prophetic: on September 20, 1840, Philemon and Cyrena were married.

When Philemon later joined the Mormon Battalion, Cyrena could not bear the separation. She and her three children, including her three-month-old baby, set out with the battalion to Fort Leavenworth, Kansas. When the battalion reached the fort on August 1, 1846, Elder Parley P. Pratt came to collect the soldiers' pay for the support of their families and advised that Philemon send his wife and children back to Winter Quarters. Acting on Elder Pratt's advice, Philemon did send Cyrena and the children back to Winter Quarters, asking fourteen-year-old Monroe Frick to drive the team for Cyrena.

Wanting to make sure they got on their way safely, Philemon traveled a day's journey with his family as they started back over two hundred miles of lonely road. Cyrena said that watching him leave the next morning to rejoin the battalion "was the hardest of all her trials" (Maynes, 338).

ELIZABETH HOWE BULLARD HYDE

Elizabeth Howe Bullard Hyde's husband, William, wrote in his journal of his enlistment with the battalion:

> I looked upon my family and then upon my aged parents
> and upon the situation of the camps in the midst of an un-
> cultivated wild country . . . and my soul revolted.
>
> But when I came to learn the mind of the Lord . . . I
> said, "Here am I, take me." (Maynes, 288)

As William marched off with the battalion, he left a pregnant Elizabeth and two daughters sheltered in a drafty wagon bed.

Soon after beginning the march, undoubtedly overwhelmed with
concern, William left the battalion and returned to Council Bluffs to
see his wife and children once more. After a brief visit with his family, William turned back toward Fort Leavenworth and continued the
march with the battalion.

A day later, William returned yet again to Council Bluffs and tar-
ried until 2 P.M. At last he gave his family a blessing and then, resigning
them into the hands of God, he left them a final time, catching up with
the battalion (see Maynes, 288).

THE GIRL I'VE LEFT BEHIND ME

I'm lonesome since I crossed the hill, And o'er the moor and valley;
Such heavy thoughts my heart do fill, since parting from my Sally,
I seek no more the fine and gay, For each does but remind me,
How swift the hours did pass away, With the girl I've left behind
me.

Oh! Ne'er shall I forget the night the stars were bright above me,
And gently lent their silvery light, when first she vowed to love me,
But now I'm bound for Brighton Camp, Kind Heaven, then pray
guide me,
And send me safely back again to the girl I've left behind me.

My mind shall still her from retain, in sleeping or in waking,
Until I see my love again, for whom my heart is breaking.
If ever I return that way, and she should not decline me,
I ever more will live and stay with the girl I've left behind me.

        —Original Battalion Song
        (Girl I've Left Behind)

UNCERTAINTY

Jesus said unto him, If thou canst believe,
all things are possible to him that believeth.
And straightway the father of the child cried out,
and said with tears, Lord, I believe;
help thou my unbelief.
—Mark 9:23–24

PAUL TAUGHT THAT MORTALITY IS as looking "through a glass darkly" (1 Cor. 13:12). How often is a sure sense of direction thrown into chaos by that which is unexpected or unjust? And how often might be repeated the words "Lord, I believe; help thou my unbelief"?

The Church members on the prairie were all converts, and many of them were young families. Their trials taxed their faith and, like the "father of a child," they felt the need for greater spiritual assurance, for deeper understanding of the divine, for a trust in the Lord that was unquestionable. The trail behind some of them was strewn with the debris of doubt and despair, and the task ahead of them seemed unbearable and unobtainable.

These early Saints were not only pioneers in traversing the plains and settling the West, they were also pioneers of thought, of faith, and of magnified trust in the Lord. They blazed philosophical trails, shaping the events that would bequeath a new identity to future generations of truth-seeking people.

Blazing trials—whether the trails lie across a continent or in the stony tables of the heart—is a long and arduous process. Testimonies did not mature in a single day; there must have been times when some of the Saints cried out, "Lord, I believe; help thou my unbelief." Transitions took time, and there were moments of uncertainty along the way.

$\mathscr{D}$rusilla $\mathscr{H}$endricks

My fury would come up and I had no language to express my feelings.
I was in a complete struggle . . .

FROM HER YOUTH, DRUSILLA DORRIS HENDRICKS treasured the Bible and had a propensity for spiritual truths. Some of those feelings were due in part to the fact that as a child of ten years, she encountered an alarming disease and a miraculous healing:

> I was taken in a severe pain in my side and for three days and nights they thought I would die. . . . I lay in great pain . . . I could not move myself. One evening I think it must have been sunset, My Mother came and asked me how I felt. I was sinking under the load I felt on me and I said, "O! Mother, raise me up" and as she raised me up the light and glory of Heaven seemed to fill the house. . . . I shouted and praised God in the name of Jesus. . . . My pain was gone. (Drusilla, 2)

Drusilla interpreted this moment as a powerful spiritual experience, and said, "I want to live to be baptized for the remission of my sins" (Drusilla, 2). When she was finally introduced to the gospel, her acceptance was instantaneous, undeniable, and enduring. She and her husband, James Hendricks, were baptized in Kentucky in 1835.

In 1838, the Hendricks family was living in Clay County, Missouri, where Drusilla and James generously offered shelter and provisions to the families that were forced out of Caldwell County after the

Haun's Mill massacre. Little did they know that the same fate of exile awaited them. And in the end, their trials included more than exile: in the Battle of Crooked River, James was shot in the neck and was permanently paralyzed from the shoulders down (see Drusilla, 12–13).

Nine years later, having lived in Quincy and then Nauvoo, Illinois, James and Drusilla and their children were settled at Winter Quarters. When the call came for men to enlist in the Mormon Battalion, Drusilla's oldest son, William, was eighteen years old and a prime recruit—but Drusilla depended on him and did not want him to join the battalion. Though James was the family patriarch, William was physically the "man of the house," and Drusilla relied on his strength.

Drusilla's dependence on William was not the only factor behind her unwillingness to comply with the request. She felt the government that was calling for William's service, and perhaps his life, had failed in protecting her family and the other Saints. She was forthright and impassioned toward the audacity of the government in making such a request:

> After driving us from our homes three times in Missouri, breaking three treaties with us, killing our husbands and children and confiscating our property and taking our land that we had paid money for . . . Thousands of us must go, in the dead of winter, no matter our sufferings, we must go or be exterminated. . . . My fury would come up and I had no language to express my feelings. I was in a complete struggle. (Drusilla, 18)

As the day of the battalion departure approached, people repeatedly asked Drusilla if her son William was going to enlist. Repeatedly, Drusilla answered, "No."

But in moments of contemplation, solemn questions—and later answers—surfaced from the deep recesses of Drusilla's heart:

> When I was alone the whisperings of the spirit would say to me, "Are you afraid to trust the God of Israel? Has He not been with you in all your trials? Has He not provided for your wants?" Then I would have to acknowledge the hand of God in all His goodness to me. (Drusilla, 18)

Drusilla recounts the morning that William left:

> William came in wet with dew from the grass and we sat
> down around the board [table] and my husband com-
> menced asking the blessing on our food, when Thomas Wil-
> liams came shouting at the top of his voice, saying "Turn
> out men, Turn out, for we do not wish to press you but we
> lack some men yet in the battalion."
>
> William raised his eyes and looked me in the face. I
> knew then that he would go. . . . I could not swallow one
> bite of breakfast but I waited on the rest thinking I might
> never have my family all together again. I had no photo-
> graph of him but I took one in my mind and said to myself,
> "If I never see you again until the morning of the resurrec-
> tion I shall know you are my child." (Drusilla, 19)

Drusilla thoughtfully added:

> I went to milk the cows. . . . I thought the cows would be
> shelter for me and I knelt down and told the Lord if He
> wanted my child to take him, only spare his life and let him
> be restored to me and to the bosom of the church. I felt it
> was all I could do. Then the voice that talked with me in the
> morning answered me saying, "It shall be done unto you as
> it was unto Abraham when he offered Isaac on the altar." I
> don't know whether I milked or not for I felt the Lord had
> spoken to me. (Drusilla, 19)

After her son marched away with the battalion, Drusilla strapped
her invalid husband into a rocking chair in a wagon and took her family west. She was reunited with her son, William, in October 1847 in
the Salt Lake Valley.

The last words of Drusilla's diary reaffirm her testimony:

> The gospel is true, I have rejoiced in it through all my trials
> for the Spirit of the Lord has buoyed me up or I should have
> failed. . . . (Raymond Family)

* * *

He lives to bless me with His love.
He lives to plead for me above . . .
He lives to comfort me when faint.
He lives to hear my soul's complaint

He lives to silence all my fears.
He lives to wipe away my tears.
He lives to calm my troubled heart.
He lives all blessings to impart.

—Hymns, *136*

Margaret L. Scott

May our heavenly father direct and protect you and in due time
return to safe home is the prayer of your sister who loves you
with undimmed affection—

LITTLE IS KNOWN OF MARGARET L. SCOTT; in fact, only two letters exist to tell of her dedication and supplication. As the soldiers of the Mormon Battalion prepared to march, Corporal James Allen Scott, Company E, wrote to his sister about his decision to enlist. His original letter does not exist, but Margaret's reply enables us to understand not only the contents of his letter, but also the treasured relationship between brother and sister:

> Tennessee Dyer City August the 30th
> Mr. J. Allen Scott
>   Dear brother I received your letter . . . and with mingled emotions of sorrow and admiration I perused its content. I would have written by the next mail, but my mind was too much agitated to write.
>   James you are aware that it is a hard trial, but I have no alternative, but to submit and calmly resign myself and my beloved brother, into the arms of our heavenly father for protection, and preservation.
>   You speak correctly when you say, that I do not understand the present movements of the church—would that I did. They are indeed strange to me. For the Church to start to leave the U.S. and stop on the way, and send 500 of her members, to bear privations, and encounter danger, in the

service of this government, is, I acknowledge, beyond my comprehension. As to protecting the church, perhaps she [the government] will, and perhaps she will not. You know how she has acted in that regard.

But, not withstanding my ignorance on the subject, I have confidence enough in your judgment to believe that you have good reasons for acting as you have done. Nevertheless I wish it were otherwise. When you write again cant you put some of the whys and wherefores on a scrap so as to give me some insight? . . .

I want you to be careful with regard to your companions—I know your disposition, you are naturally free and rather unguarded in your Conversation, which gives designing men an opportunity to take advantage of your simplicity. You have placed yourself in [a] tight place and I know it will require more self control than you are accustomed to get along.

I scarce know what to say to you, you have acted so differently to what I expected. But I would not discourage you now. I want you to stand to your resolution, viz., to act uprightly and acquit yourself honorably—-you tell me that your Battalion is the army of Israel and I trust it is and also that you are the Servants of God. . . .

The winter is coming. Be sure to procure under clothing if possible and take good care of your health as circumstances will admit of, be temperate in all things. You know that nature has her laws which if transgressed you will be punished—

And I pray our Heavenly Father that his choicest blessings may rest on your Battalion collectively and on you individually. I am much pleased that you have prayers so regularly in your Crowd. If prayer is attended to throughout the campaign in faith and humility I think you will be preserved—

I peruse your letters with satisfaction and profit. I am pleased with the manner in which you write. But my dear brother the more I see to admire the harder it is to part with you but I am determined with the aid of the holy spirit to try to bear up under it, hoping that it will be all for the best, though I can't understand it now. . . .

When I consider the dangers to which you are exposed and the hardships you must undergo and the length of time before you are free, it is almost insupportable, but when I reflect whose you are, a gleam of hope inspires me with courage, and I feel like we'll meet again and spend some happy hours together; if you write often it will help to support me.

Next to your God, endeavour to gain the good will of your officers if they try to be good men and obey them you must whether good or bad. Are your Captains all Elders? I want a particular account of your captain. May our heavenly father direct and protect you and in due time return you safe home is the prayer of your sister who loves you with undimmed affection—

—Margrett L. Scott (Bigler/Bagley, 66–68)

Margaret's brother passed away February 5, 1847. Stationed with the sick detachment of the battalion in Pueblo, Colorado, James Allen Scott died of an acute but unnamed disease. In response to this news, Margaret wrote another letter, this time to President Brigham Young:

Tennessee Dyer City Sept the 17th 1848
Mr. Brigham Young—
Respected brother in Christ.
Can you, though the multiplicity of business necessarily involving on [sic] you, by your high station in the Church of Christ, can you I repeat, find leisure to read these lines and reply to them?

My brother James A. Scott, my only brother, the Idol of my heart, around whom was entwined all my sisterly affections, has fallen a victim to the cold grasp of death, and now his body rests at Pueblo.

In the spring of 1846 br. James went to Nauvoo. . . , (He and I having previously connected ourselves with the church.) He continued at Nauvoo until June. . . .

By this time his mind was satisfied relative to the latter-day work, and he was only coming after me (his only sister) to go on with the emigrants. When he arrived at the Bluffs the call was made for Volunteers, and he responded to the call. But not until he had consulted you privately on the subject. He informed me by letter that your advice publicly and privately was go. Also that Elder Kimball the second in the kingdom said that if they went in faith, they should be like the sons of Moroni, [Helaman] not one of them should fall. . . .

Well I have good reason to believe that my brother went in faith. I have in my possession five letters written after he volunteered. In them I have evidence, that he firmly believed he was in the path of duty, and that he would be preserved, and permitted to return for me—I am informed by letter from those that were with him that his conduct was exemplary and his faith firm.—

Now brother Young, Why has he fallen? And he in the path of duty, under the direction of the church, fallen contrary to his faith and expectations. I repeat why why has he fallen?

He was young, his talents above the common order, his education tolerably good, his conduct exemplary through life. And yet he is gone in the bloom of youth, to try the realities of the eternal world, fallen too in a land of strangers far far from those he loved.

Will you satisfy my mind concerning his apparently untimely end. . . . To you I turn for consolation and light. Believing that you are in possession of that wisdom which cometh from above and that you will take pleasure in enlightening the darkened mind, and binding up the bleeding heart of a bereaved sister. . . .

If you write, any information or advice that wisdom may dictate will be gratefully received. If you wish information relative to my br[other']s conduct, I refer you [to] elder Levi Hancock, Capts. Higgins, Hunt, Brown and Davis and many other of the battalion—I Close by again requesting you to sympathise with me in my bereavement, and grant my request, and thereby dispel the cloud of darkness that envelopes my mind.

May the eternal Father bless you with light and wisdom, and influence you to answer this immediately is the prayer of her whose heart is opprest with sorrow

    —In the bonds of the new and Everlasting Covenant
    Margaret L. Scott (Bigler/Bagley, 424–425)

There is no record of a reply to Margaret's letter in the Brigham Young collection. It should be noted, however, that Brigham Young's office did not begin to log outgoing correspondence until November 22, 1851, so it is possible that President Young sent a reply to Margaret that was not registered (see Bigler/Bagley, 425).

Margaret's brother, James, appears to have been worthy of the high esteem that Margaret placed upon him. Drawing on her compilation of soldiers' diaries, Norma Ricketts wrote:

> James Scott died February 5 after a short period of severe suffering. The description of this funeral affords an idea of the respect and honors the deceased received. Not all deaths were written about in such detail. (Ricketts, 248–249)

Battalion soldier John Steele wrote of James's funeral:

> A number of our sisters accompanied the corpse. A company of fine looking soldiers accompanied the corpse with shouldered arms under the command of Lieutenant Willis. When the body was laid in the grave, Brother Chase said a few remarks upon the deceased. . . . "He is gone to the courts above to carry news respecting our battalion. . . . In the morning of the first resurrection he will come forth for he has fell asleep in Jesus." After that the soldiers fired three vollies of musquetry and then retired, leaving the pall bearers to cover up the grave. (Ricketts, 249)

Prose Written by Margaret's brother, James Allen Scott

Pass by,
days of subjection to Gentile tyrants,
and let the oppressed Mormon soldier,
who under unparalleled circumstances,
voluntarily,
for the sake & to obtain a resting place for his brethren,
made a sacrifice
of feedings of both body and Mind
& yielded the inducements of worldly interests
(at least for the present) to
a sense of duty,
feelings of love
& to obtain far in the west a home for the Saints.

Eight months more & we meet those for whom we suffered . . .
& in connection with them raise our houses,
cultivate our soil,
live once more upon the good things of life,
build our God a house
& enjoy the sweets of Liberty
undisturbed by mobs. (Ricketts, 313)

Alice Clayton Martin

The battalion March, a three-year mission in Scotland, and then the ill-timed handcart company . . .

ALICE CLAYTON WAS BORN IN Walton, Penworthen, England—the same town in which she met Edward Martin. In 1840, they were married in Preston, Lancashire, during a time when missionaries in Great Britain were preaching to large groups of working-class people. One of the missionary areas, Preston was a large industrialized textile community of sixty thousand workers. When Alice and Edward came into contact with the missionaries, they felt the truthfulness of the gospel and joined the Church (see Maynes, 322). The following story, written by Roxanne Grey, is based on the facts of Alice Clayton Martin's life:

Alice and Mary Ellen were quietly sewing in the lamplight of the Martins' small home. The two had been diligently working for weeks, preparing for the return of their husband and father. Mary Ellen did as she was told, knowing that if she were to ask too many questions the worried and hollowed look would reappear on her mother's face. They had scrubbed the house raw, tended to the garden, mended the bedding, and were now sewing a new outfit for Edward. After so many years, a new outfit was sure to be appreciated.

Edward had not seen his wife and daughter for more than three years. After marching with the battalion, he served a mission for the Lord in Scotland, after which he was then asked to lead a handcart company of Saints on his way back to the Salt Lake Valley.

Alice willed each carefully placed stitch to take her mind far from the accounts that she received weekly of her husband's travels. It was difficult to root the worry from her heart; the Martin Handcart Company had encountered so many obstacles as they made the journey west. Because members of the company had been unable to purchase the right building supplies, the handcarts had fallen apart on the rough terrain. And leaving late in the season, the Company had also been trapped in severe blizzards and freezing temperatures near a place called Devil's Gate.

Just recently President Brigham Young had sent wagons to rescue the pioneers. Alice had heard the Saints were stranded in the snow and destitute of supplies and food when the rescue teams finally reached them. The rescuers sent word back to President Young that it was the saddest sight that they had ever seen.

Alice waited, quietly.

Every night she gathered as much news as she could from those in town before retreating to her bedside and falling to her knees. She humbly asked her Heavenly Father to look after her husband. Life had already dealt her so many harsh blows. She could not forget the night in the wagon box at Winter Quarters when her son, Edward John, was born and died before morning. Alice had regained her strength but two more of her children had not. When Edward returned from walking 6,120 miles with the battalion, only she and young Mary Ellen were standing there to greet him.

Now, as Alice waited for him to return from the handcart trek, she carefully folded the hem of her husband's new pants and said another silent prayer.

Edward did return from the trek, though he had lost fifty pounds and was extremely weak. It took a considerable amount of time for him to regain his strength. Thanks to Alice's and Mary Ellen's careful and affectionate tending, he was eventually able to fit into the new outfit they had prepared for him.

The Martin Handcart Company

WHEN ALICE CLAYTON MARTIN PARTED with her husband—first as he marched away with the Mormon Battalion and again when he left on a mission to Scotland— she had no way of knowing that he would also be the leader of a handcart company.

After hearing the harrowing stories of the Willie Handcart Company, which arrived in the Salt Lake Valley November 9, 1856, she would wait another three long weeks for her husband, Edward Martin, to return on November 30 (see Martin Handcart Company).

That summer, more than thirteen hundred Saints from England pulled handcarts across the plains. The first three of the five companies were successful and arrived in the Salt Lake Valley without incident. But the last two companies—the Willie and Martin companies—left too late in the season. Another serious complication was that the carts were constructed of green wood and did not stand up to the strenuous journey west. When the Saints finally reached Wyoming, they found themselves at the mercy of immense rugged mountains barricaded in snows sometimes six feet deep and ravaged by freezing winds of up to sixty miles an hour.

Of the 576 people who left with the Martin Handcart Company, 145 did not survive. The journey of this company was one of the most soul-piercing events in the history of the Church.

As general conference convened on October 5, President Brigham Young spoke to the congregation:

I will now give this people the subject and the text for ...
the conference. It is this: ... many of our brethren and sisters are on the plains with handcarts, and probably many of
them are now seven hundred miles from this place, and they
must be brought here; we must send assistance to them. The
text will be, "to get them here." ...

I call upon the Bishops this day. I shall not wait until
tomorrow, nor until the next day, for 60 good mule teams
and 12 or 15 wagons. ... Also, 12 tons of flour, and 40 good
teamsters. I will tell you that all your faith, religion, and the
profession of religion will never save one soul of you in the
Celestial Kingdom of God, unless you carry out just such
principles as I am now teaching you. Go and bring in those
people now on the plains. (Kelly, 308–309)

Within two days, wagons loaded with donated food, clothing, and
supplies were moving eastward. It took almost two months to bring
the stranded members of the Martin Company to the relief of the Salt
Lake Valley. Many of the Saints who walked into the valley in November said of their handcart experience that it was the moment in time in
which their deepest strains of faith were forged by virtue of complete
and all-embracing dependence on the Lord.

As for Alice, her faith was forged when she chose prayer over doubt.

MIRACLES

ACCORDING TO THE BIBLE DICTIONARY, miracles are a response to faith (see Bible Dictionary, 732–733). Because of their faith, the men and women of the Mormon Battalion witnessed many "mercies and miracles" as the Lord responded to that faith, blessing them with tender mercies that defy ordinary explanation. As confirmed by Elder David A. Bednar, such "tender mercies" of the Lord are not random coincidences; instead, they are highly individualized blessings, assurances, supports, and spiritual gifts given to us by and through the Savior (see "The Tender Mercies of the Lord," *Ensign*, May 2005).

In very real, very heart-touching, and very life-changing ways, the Lord miraculously reached down and touched the lives of individual Saints, manifesting both His boundless love for them and His intimate knowledge of their personal wants and needs.

Nothing could separate them from the love of God:

> *For I am persuaded, that neither death, nor life, nor angels,*
> *nor principalities, nor powers, nor things present,*
> *nor things to come,*
> *Nor height, or depth, nor any other creature,*
> *shall be able to separate us from the love of God,*
> *which is in Jesus Christ our Lord.*
> *—Rom. 8:38–39*

Nothing could stop His miracles from pouring down upon them:

Wherefore, my beloved brethren,
have miracles ceased because Christ ascended into heaven,
and hath sat down on the right hand of God,
to claim of the Father his rights of mercy
which he hath upon the children of men? . . .
Behold I say unto you, Nay;
neither have angels ceased to minister
unto the children of men.
—Moro. 7:27–29

Seviah Cunningham Egbert

When Seviah looked up, the stranger was nowhere to be seen . . .

SEVIAH CUNNINGHAM'S HOMELAND WAS CANADA. Her mother, Sarah Stevens Cunningham, died when Seviah was a small child. While living in Ontario, Seviah's father, Charles Peter Cunningham, accepted the gospel and moved the family to Missouri.

In Jackson County, Missouri, the persecutions were aggressive and combative. In 1839, when Seviah was only ten years old, the Cunningham family was driven from Jackson County into Caldwell County. Seviah always remembered the black, charred earth where her father's crops—just ready to be harvested—had been burned to the ground.

The Cunningham family moved to Nauvoo in 1840, where Seviah was baptized four years later at the age of fifteen.

During the time Seviah and her family lived in Nauvoo, the temple was under construction. Robert Cowden Egbert, a young man who was working on the temple, found himself captivated by Seviah and married the beautiful seventeen-year-old girl on April 1, 1846 (see Maynes, 173). The marriage took place only three short months before Robert marched away with the battalion; Seviah stayed behind with Robert's family.

The seasons passed. Two years went by, and still Seviah had not received a letter from her husband. Not having heard from him since he marched away with the battalion, she wondered if she was ever going to see him again. When Robert's parents decided to move west, Seviah informed them that she would be traveling with them. Independent and as self-sufficient as possible, Seviah drove her own team of oxen; her only request to her male relatives was that they help her yoke and unyoke the animals.

The cross-continental trek was not easy for anyone; it was especially hard for a woman alone. The endless prairie often became dreadfully lonely, and occasionally prairie dust was caked to Seviah's skin where tears had trailed down her face. Just when her faith was perhaps feeling fragmented, splintering into various doubts, the Lord responded to her fears with mercy and miracles:

> One day when [Seviah] was especially sad, she looked out in the distance and saw a man on a horse coming from the opposite direction. She thought this to be strange as [they had seen no other travelers for hundreds of miles]. The stranger was coming directly toward her. . . . He came up to the wagon and asked if she was Robert Egbert's wife. She replied that she was. He told her: "I have a letter from Robert for you."
>
> She took the letter and saw that it was written in Robert's handwriting. The letter told her that he was well, and would meet her at the head of the Sweetwater in Wyoming. She wished to inquire further about Robert from the traveler, however, when she looked up he was nowhere to be seen. . . .
>
> She placed the letter in her basket. Later when she decided to read it again, it was nowhere to be found. . . .
>
> After the company had arrived at the Sweetwater, Seviah immediately looked for Robert, but could not find him. Meanwhile Robert rode into the camp from the west. He was not looking for Seviah as he assumed that he would find her in Iowa. As he was looking over the teams and outfits to see if he might recognize any of them, he came upon one team that he did recognize; he thought that it looked like his own. He meandered up close to the wagon and looked inside. He was greatly surprised to see Seviah, however, she was not surprised to see him. She told him about the letter she had received from the stranger.
>
> He told her he had not written a letter to her. . . . They both marveled over this strange experience, but Seviah silently rejoiced over the happiness that it had brought to her. (Maynes, 174, 175)

Seviah and Robert arrived in the Salt Lake Valley in the fall of 1848. Three years later, in the spring of 1851, they were called by President Brigham Young to go with apostles Charles C. Rich and Amasa Lyman to establish a settlement in San Bernardino, California.

Both Seviah and Robert were unfaltering stalwarts in the Church. At a testimony meeting held on November 1, 1863, Robert stood and spoke about his love for the gospel of Jesus Christ. He also told the congregation of his impending death. That night he went home, became ill, and died the following morning.

When Robert died, Seviah was left with a family of seven children and was expecting her eighth. She returned to Utah and raised her children, working as a seamstress—carding and spinning yarn, weaving cloth, and making rugs, carpets, and buckskin gloves for men. She earned a living for her family and did whatever she could to make their lives comfortable and happy (see Maynes, 176).

FAVORITE WIND

Winds blow night and day
    Whispering their ancient tunes
    To all who listen.

Winds are not alike.
    Some roar with all their might;
    Others sigh so low.

Some winds have power
    To move ships on the ocean
    Or turn a windmill.

A wind that soothes
    As it whispers in the pines—
    My favorite wind.

—Gladys LaVeryl Hall Cleavinger

Clarissa Reed Hancock

Mother reached down on the side to get her old shoes
and held up a new pair . . .

WHILE WORKING IN JOSEPH SMITH's home, Clarissa Reed became acquainted with Levi Hancock; they were married on March 29, 1833. Levi was the son of a Revolutionary War veteran and a relative of John Hancock, the first man to sign the Declaration of Independence. Blessed with the same bold blood that flowed fiercely through his ancestor's veins, Levi possessed a resolute will that enabled him to face down danger of every kind.

Clarissa, his helpmate and companion, was his courageous equal. During a period of unbridled hostility toward the Saints, Clarissa and twenty other women were gathered in Lucy Mack Smith's home. One of the women asked, "Now that the mob has taken our guns, what shall we do?" Clarissa fearlessly replied, "We can do as the Carthage women did when the Romans took the arms off their husbands; we can pull the hair out of our heads so the menfolks can make bowstrings" (Maynes, 229).

In his journal, Clarissa's son Mosiah told of his parents' bravery when describing the day the mob came to Far West to act on Governor Boggs' extermination order:

> The night before the surrender, mother had run 250 bullets for Father's musket. Father and his brothers and a few others did not give up their weapons. There were sixteen guns that were not surrendered. The owners, taking their sixteen

guns into the thicket, caused more consternation against the mob than all the mobbers' guns caused against the Saints. It is a fact which should be remembered; the Hancock brothers, Levi, Joseph, and Solomon, with their guns, guarded and fed 600 men, women, and children while camped in the woods after they had been driven from their homes. (Maynes, 229)

A mob later entered the Hancocks' next homestead, giving the family three days to leave Missouri. Having no recourse, Levi rigged up a cart that he filled with corn, and the family abandoned yet another home—this time in the dead of winter. Son Mosiah described the scene:

> The snow was deep enough to take me to the middle of the thigh, and I was barefooted and in my shirt tail. Mother had made me two shirts in Kirtland, and the shirt I had on stuck to me, or rather, I stuck to the shirt.
>
> We had old Tom hitched to the cart, and Father drove the horse and carried the rifle on his shoulder. Mother followed the cart carrying my little brother Francis Marion in her arms. I tried to follow in her tracks.
>
> We finally stopped to rest and get something to eat, but Mother said she could not stand it much longer. She cried, and Father said: "Cheer up, Clarissa, for I prophesy in the name of the Lord Jesus Christ you shall have a pair of shoes delivered to you before long, in a remarkable manner." After we had made our fire and eaten of our roasted corn on the cob, Mother reached down on the side to get her old shoes and held up a new pair. Father answered, "Clarissa, did I not tell you that God would provide to you a pair in a remarkable manner?" (Maynes, 230)

Levi purchased land in Nauvoo; Clarissa and Levi were sealed in the Nauvoo Temple on January 16, 1846.

But their respite in Nauvoo came to a sudden end when a mob arrived suddenly at their home, bellowing with wanton insults, wielding torches, and discharging unrestrained gunfire. Grasping six children tightly in her arms, Clarissa was forced to stand back and watch another home burn to the ground.

Sorting through the smoldering ashes for what little had not been destroyed, the Hancock family loaded up their wagon with what meager supplies they could salvage from the wreckage and set out for Iowa. Mosiah wrote about their travels:

> It was quite late when we left. Besides we had rain every day while there. Oh, the storms. When we did get ready to start, father would take us on one day's travel; then the next day he would go back and get Grandmother Reed and Uncle Levi and Uncle Ira. And father would bring them all up so we would all be together at night. Thus, father traveled, and kept the two families along by traveling the road over three times until we caught up with the Pioneers at Counsel Point. We got there just in time for President Young, Kimball, and Richards, to come and choose father to go and spiritually preside over the Mormon Battalion. (Maynes, 231)

While Levi was away on the march with the battalion, Clarissa set out for the Salt Lake Valley with her family—along with twenty-seven bushels of cornmeal, fifteen pounds of flour, two pigs, a dog, and a cat. Her brother drove one team and Mosiah drove the other, except when the men went searching for game, at which time Clarissa handled the team on her own.

By the time they reached Cache Cave, Clarissa and Levi were finally reunited. They arrived together in the Salt Lake Valley on August 3, 1848.

Margaret Jane Willis Willis

Margaret knelt down next to her wagon . . .

REFLECTING ON HIS CHOICE OF a companion, William Wesley Willis said of Margaret Jane Willis, "I couldn't have chosen a more beautiful, healthy, or intelligent girl anywhere" (Maynes, 328). Second cousins, Margaret and William were married March 29, 1833. Thirteen years later, William marched away with the battalion, leaving Margaret with seven children. The following story, written by Roxanne Grey, is based on a true incident that occurred during Margaret's journey to the Salt Lake Valley with her children:

The swelling was getting worse. John Henry lay in the back of the wagon with his leg propped up on a box. Today he was not even able to stand on it.

When John Henry first noticed the swelling in his leg, he assured his mother that he would be just fine. She had watched him limping as he unyoked the oxen and led them out into the fields. She feared that John Henry was trying not to worry her—which made her worry even more. She knew that her son, only thirteen years of age, felt it his responsibility to take care of the family since his father left with the battalion.

This morning, unable to leave the wagon box, he could not yoke the oxen. His face was pinched and worried, and Margaret knew he was trying to keep back tears.

"Mama, I'm sorry," he said. "I'm sorry I let you down."

Margaret climbed up into the wagon box and grabbed his hand.

"This is not your fault, John Henry."

She kissed his forehead and stepped down from the wagon. She could hear the rest of camp preparing to continue on. The women were packing pots and pans, and the men and boys were yoking the oxen for another day's journey. Margaret knew she could not stop and wait for John Henry's leg to heal, but she also knew that she could not care for the cattle without his help. If they did not leave with the rest of the company, they would be left behind on the prairie.

Straight away Margaret knelt down next to her wagon. She closed her eyes intently and tried to tune out the noises of the camp. Her children climbed up next to their older brother in the wagon, and the camp continued to buzz around her as Margaret prayed.

When she finished her prayer, she resumed packing the wagon for the day's journey. She put out the campfire, loaded the food and pots, made sure the children were dressed, and carefully laid the baby in the wagon box wrapped in a thick quilt. As she was strapping in the butter churn, a thought came to her mind.

Go find Elder Smith.

Margaret did not think twice; she ran quickly across the camp. Elder Ashael Smith, a relative of the Prophet Joseph Smith, was yoking his own oxen when she found him. He followed her back to the wagon, where John Henry lay still. She paused momentarily to join her spirit with the words of the elder's prayer of healing.

She continued her work. She was feeding the cattle when she saw John Henry walk over and begin to yoke the oxen. Leading the team to the wagon, he walked steadily on two legs.

Margaret dropped to her knees in prayer.

"Thank you, Dear Lord."

In Closing

THREATENED BY MOBS, THE EARLY members of the Church somehow found strength to defend themselves. Facing the harshness of the environment without a roof overhead, still they pushed forward. Burying loved ones and neighbors, one after another, they pushed on for the promise of happiness in Zion. They heeded the prophet's call to not wilt away in defeat but to stand and persevere.

After being asked to trust the Lord, the Mormon Battalion did just that, leaving wives and children to His tender mercies. The women were asked to eke out what living they could without the help of their cherished eternal companions. In the face of all that was hardest for them to bear—death, poverty, disease, and being stranded in a wilderness—these women survived. They endured. They fought the struggles of existence, and they prevailed.

The women who were left behind on the prairie in July of 1846 are important strands in the fabric of Church history. Only a small number of women are represented in this book but their stories represent those of several hundred women, to whom is owed a deepest debt of gratitude.

The stories of these women have been arranged into sections denoting loss, triumph, sacrifice, blessings, friendship, romance, uncertainty, and miracles. But in the end, *all* of the stories of *all* of these women are stories of loss and triumph, of sacrifice and blessings, of friendship and romance, of uncertainty and miracles . . . as are our stories.

From the vantage point of mortality, we cannot behold all of the themes of our lives. We cannot see how all of the threads intertwine. As it was for the women on the plains, it is hard for us to walk, work, and wait, not knowing conclusions or outcomes. We will be able to behold the panoramic designs of our lives only when the events of mortality are no longer interpreted by where lies the thin border we call death.

The overall pattern of our existence will reveal the greatest story of love ever told or imagined. For no matter how the events of our lives are interpreted while here on earth, if we have chosen to sanctify our souls through the love and sacrifice of our Savior, we will look out over a new and glorious expanse where "eye hath not seen, nor ear heard, neither have entered into the heart of man, the things that God hath prepared for them who love Him" (1 Cor. 2:9).

EPILOGUE

IN THE SUMMER OF 2003, I was elated by a proposal originated by R. Don Oscarson. His vision was to share through dance and film the stories of pioneer women who were left on the plains when the men marched away as soldiers in the Mormon Battalion.

Don had previously written and worked on a BYU production telling the stories of the Mormon Battalion, and he received the impression that the stories of the women needed to be told. As I began work on the project, I encountered a treasured moment of spiritual sisterhood.

After laboring on the project for a year, my student research assistant and I were driving from Provo to Salt Lake City to visit the LDS Church Archives. I was exhausted at the time and found myself thinking that although this project was one of utmost importance, I was not the person to undertake it and bring it to fruition. I committed myself to thinking of a capable person who could complete this project with the high degree of care and expertise that it deserved.

Upon arrival at the LDS Church Archives, my research assistant went upstairs to investigate some references. I remained on the main floor, waiting for a select book to be brought to me. I was sitting alone in a small glassed-in area, engaged in deep concentration on who should be entrusted with this valuable project.

As I was fixed upon that thought, I became aware that the small glass room was filled with women . . . many women. I was astutely aware of one woman in particular who was standing just behind me and to my left.

I recognized that these women were the spirits of those whose lives I was researching. My eyes welled with tears as I realized the sacred nature of the opportunity that lay before me.

As I tried to comprehend the experience that had overcome me, a gentleman walked into the area and placed a book on the reading table. The women in the room seemed to dissipate, but the woman standing next to me, the one whose life story I was currently researching, remained. Confident that I would be successful in my research, I began to examine the musty pages for information. Unfortunately, the book was not helpful.

At that point, my research assistant returned from upstairs and informed me that the library was closing. Empty-handed, we headed to the LDS Family History Library.

At the Family History Library, my assistant and I began searching the databases and were thrilled when we found a microfilm containing the autobiography of the woman whose life we were researching.

Once we obtained the microfilm, we were promptly beset by a chain of perplexing complications that required us to do nothing more than solve problems for several hours. When we finally accessed the file, we were mesmerized, and with tearful eyes we began to read through a straightforward but poetic autobiography written by this woman.

It was now close to 10 p.m. We made our way to an office area to render the microfilm copy to a paper copy. While surrounded by computers, copiers, and assorted offices noises, and while my eyes were fixed on the copier, the spirit of this same woman came and stood next to me again. She remained with me the entire time it took to copy her story. I felt her warmth as the sweetness of her spirit permeated my entire being.

In the moment of this encounter, I recognized that our unique individuality is profoundly spiritual, transcending physical appearance or voice. And I learned that these pioneers care about us and are deeply involved in the day-to-day events of our present lives.

I don't know if I have done justice to this project. I do hope I have shared at least something that is worthy of these beautiful pioneer women.

Be that as it may, I believe that these pioneers belong to the wide populations of the world. When I served a mission, I observed that converts to the Church from all over the world seem to feel a direct and personal connection to these remarkable people. Members of the Church everywhere seem to regard the early Saints as their own progenitors. I marvel that so few people seem to have laid a foundation for so many.

Therefore, my experience with these pioneer women is not my own. It belongs to all who reverence our connection to these progenitors and all who will treasure their words and experiences. It belongs to all who will hear their testimonies.

THE WOMEN

Nancy Reeder Walker Alexander
Born: December 8, 1817, Dayton, Ohio
Married: September 14, 1834, Winchester, Indiana
Died: January 28, 1847, Winter Quarters, Nebraska
Husband: Horace Martin Alexander, Private/Corporal, Company B

Sarah Beriah Fiske Allen
Born: September 1, 1819, Potsdam, New York
Married: December 25, 1837
Died: June 12, 1891, Logan, Utah
Husband: Ezra Healy Allen, Musician, Company C

Amy Ann Marble Babcock
Born: February 14, 1826, Huntsburg, Ohio
Married: 1844, Nauvoo, Illinois
Died: September 1862, Price, Utah
Husband: Lorenzo Babcock, Private, Company C

Elizabeth Harris Browett
Born: June 16, 1813, Sandhurst, England
Married: June 2, 1844, England
Died: March 4, 1899, Kaysville, Utah
Husband: Daniel Browett, Corporal and Sergeant, Company E

Jane Draper Bulkley
Born: June 7, 1825, Laborough, Canada
Married: January 7, 1844, Hancock County, Illinois
Died: December 27, 1883, Springville, Utah
Husband: Newman Bulkley, Private, Company E

Emily Abbott Bunker
Born: September 19, 1827, Dansville, New York
Married: February 9, 1846, Nauvoo, Illinois
Died: February 8, 1913, Panguitch, Utah
Husband: Edward Bunker, Private, Company E

Clarrisa Lora Jones Canfield
Born: July 6, 1815, Richland, New York
Married: 1844, Nauvoo, Illinois
Died: November 27, 1892, West Jordan, Utah
Husband: Cyrus Culver Canfield, Lieutenant, Company D

Jane Louisa Jones Canfield
Born: October 17, 1812, Paris, New York
Married: October 9, 1841, Kirtland, Ohio
Died: October 25, 1872
Husband: Cyrus Culver Canfield, Lieutenant, Company D

Sarah Ann Bean Casper
Born: October 31, 1828, Bellville, Ohio
Married: August 29, 1844, Quincy, Illinois
Died: April 24, 1882, Salt Lake City, Utah
Husband: William Wallace Casper, Private, Company A

Mammy Chloe
Born: Unknown
Died: Unknown
Close friend and attendant to Mary Lee Bland Ewell

Sarah Ann Arterbury Church
Born: May 4, 1824, Dallas County, Alabama
Married: December 19, 1844, Perry County, Alabama
Died: July 29, 1889, St. George, Utah
Husband: Haden Wells Church, Private, Company B

Polly Matilda Merrill Colton
Born: October 15, 1817, Smithfield, New York
Married: July 3, 1833, Shelby, Michigan
Died: August 13, 1891, Vernal, Utah
Husband: Philander Colton, Private, Company B
Son: Charles Edwin Colton, Officer's aide

Mary Bettice Compton
Born: December 20, 1814, Wilson County, Tennessee
Married: January 13, 1832, Wilson County, Tennessee
Died: August 5, 1887, Farmington, Utah
Husband: Allen Compton, Private, Company D

Pheby Jane Ferguson Cummings
Born: May 21, 1815, Plattsburg, Vermont
Married: July 5, 1833, Michigan
Died: November 5, 1902, Millville, Utah
Husband: George Washington Cummings, Private, Company E

Seviah Cunningham Egbert
Born: October 16, 1829, Woodstock, Ontario, Canada
Married: April 1, 1846
Died: April 27, 1913, Granite, Utah
Husband: Robert Cowden Egbert, Private, Company A

Polly Pierce Knight Elmer
Born: April 29, 1788, Hancock, New Hampshire
Married: September 23, 1835
Died: *Not known*
Husband: Elijah Elmer, Sergeant, Company C

Mary Lee Bland Ewell
Born: November 1, 1817, Cumberland County, Kentucky
Married: November 30, 1834, Carroll County, Missouri
Died: May 24, 1898, Santaquin, Utah
Husband: William Ewell, Private, Company E

Mary Bingham Freeman
Born: April 1, 1820, St. Johnsbury, Vermont
Married: April 17, 1844, Nauvoo, Illinois
Died: September 25, 1893, Ogden, Utah
Husband: Elijah Norman Freeman, Private, Company B

Mary Hedrick Garner
Born: September 25, 1811, Rowan County, North Carolina
Married: April 4, 1830, Rowan County, North Carolina
Died: March 3, 1892, Ogden, Utah
Husband: Phillip Garner, Private, Company B

Elizabeth Ann Meyers Glines
Born: February 4, 1831, Bucyrus, Ohio
Married: December 20, 1845, Nauvoo, Illinois
Died: November 3, 1876, Salt Lake City, Utah
Husband: James Harvey Glines, Battalion Staff as Sgt. Major

Clarissa Reed Hancock
Born: December 18, 1814, Acworth, New Hampshire
Married: March 29, 1833, Kirtland, Ohio
Died: January 17, 1860, Salt Lake City, Utah
Husband: Levi Ward Hancock, Sr., Musician, Company E

Sarah Elizabeth Reynolds Haskell
Born: June 13, 1796, Unity, Maine
Married: 1816, Vermont
Died: November 21, 1880, Payson, Utah
Husband: George Niles Haskell, Private, Company B

Drusilla Dorris Hendricks
Born: February 8, 1810, Sumner County, Tennessee
Married: James Hendricks, May 31, 1827
Died: May 20, 1881, Richmond, Utah
Son: William Dorris Hendricks, Private, Company D

Sarah Stuart Howell
Born: January 15, 1815, Gallatin Sumner County, Tennessee
Married: July 5, 1835, Tennessee
Died: October 10, 1886, Clifton, Idaho
Husband: Thomas Charles Davis Howell, Private, Company E

Eliza Collins Hunsaker
Born: March 5, 1817, Louisville, Kentucky
Married: January 3, 1833, Quincy, Illinois
Died: October 13, 1888, Brigham City, Utah
Husband: Abraham Hunsaker, Private, Sergeant, Company D

Kiziah Brown Hunter
Born: December 10, 1808, Franklin, Kentucky
Married: December 1827, St. Louis City, Missouri
Died: After 1877, Los Angeles, California
Husband: Jesse Divined Hunter, Captain, Company B
Son: William Hunter, Musician, Company B

Mary Ann Hunter
Born: December 15, 1825, West Vincent, Pennsylvania
Married: November 18, 1843, Nauvoo, Illinois
Died: November 20, 1914, Grantsville, Utah
Husband: Edward Hunter, Private, Company B

Elizabeth Howe Bullard Hyde
Born: October 2, 1813, Holliston, Massachusetts
Married: February 23, 1842, Nauvoo, Illinois
Died: November 24, 1914, Cache County, Utah
Husband: William Hyde, Sergeant, Company B

Mary Ann Hedrick Jameson
Born: July 9, 1801, Perry, Ohio
Married: October 12, 1823, Ohio
Died: June 15, 1850, Kanesville, Iowa
Husband: Charles Jameson, Private, Company E
Daughter: Mary Ann Jameson Hirons, Laundress, Company D
Son-in-Law: James Hirons, Private, Company D

Ann Ratcliff Karren
Born: November 1, 1815, Little Crosby, England
Married: May 11, 1833, Formbly, England
Died: January 8, 1886, Provo, Utah
Husband: Thomas Karren, Private, Company E

Ann Faragher Kelly
Born: February 19, 1820, Marown, England
Married: July 19, 1846, Council Bluffs, Iowa
Died: January 3, 1880, American Fork, Utah
Husband: William Edward Kelly, Private, Company E

Alice Clayton Martin
Born: March 28, 1816, Penworthen, England
Married: 1840, Preston, Lancashire, England
Died: April 3, 1859, Buried Salt Lake County, Utah
Husband: Edward Martin, Corporal, Company C

Lucretia Charlotte Bracken Maxwell
Born: December 6, 1823, Rush County, Indiana
Married: November 26, 1840, Shawneetown, Illinois
Died: August 26, 1893, Buried in Colonia, Oaxaca, Mexico
Husband: William Bailey Maxwell, Private, Company D

Mary Jane Morris McCarty
Born: April 11, 1819, Circleville, Ohio
Married: April 30, 1843, Nauvoo, Illinois

Died: December 4, 1893, Ogden, Utah
Husband: Nelson McCarty, Private, Company B

Clarinda Bartholomew McCullough
Born: June 4, 1815, Dryden, New York
Married: January 9, 1834, Evans, New York
Died: July 12, 1847, Florence, Nebraska
Husband: Levi Hamilton McCullough, Private, Company C

Cyrena Dustin Merrill
Born: January 6, 1817, Le Roy, New York
Married: September 20, 1840, Nauvoo, Illinois
Died: February 3, 1906, Safford, Arizona
Husband: Philemon Christopher Merrill, 3rd Lieutenant, Company B

Catherine Ann Williams Owens
Born: December 11, 1819, Kanawha County, West Virginia
Married: 1837, Franklin County, Ohio
Died: May 6, 1886, Smithfield, Utah
Husband: Robert Owens, Private, Company B

Elizabeth Alden Pettegrew
Born: October 14, 1791, Claremont, New Hampshire
Married: 1816, New Hampshire
Died: July 16, 1858, Salt Lake City, Utah
Husband: David Pettegrew, Private, Company E
Son: James Phineas Pettegrew, Private, Company D

Margaret Robison Phelps
Born: May 13, 1819, Tunkannock, Pennsylvania
Married: November 15, 1835, Susquehanna County, Pennsylvania
Died: March 3, 1892, Oakley City, Idaho
Husband: Alva Phelps, Private, Company E

Clarinda Cutler Raymond
Born: January 9, 1827, Amboy, New York

Married: 1845, Nauvoo, Illinois
Died: September 24, 1862, Smithfield, Utah
Husband: Alonso Pearis Raymond, Private, Company D

Wealthy Richards
Born: September 6, 1786
Married: Phinehas Richards
Died: November 25, 1874
Son: Joseph William Richards, Musician, Company A

Mary Napier Rowe
Born: March 30, 1823, Kilsyth, Lanarkshire, Scotland
Married: Date Unknown
Died: March 4, 1902, Mt. Pleasant, Utah
Husband: Caratat Conderset Rowe, Private, Company A

Margaret L. Scott
Information not available
Brother: James Allen Scott, Corporal, Company E

Lucretia Haws Sessions
Born: November 22, 1802, Logan County, Kentucky
Married: April 14, 1821, White County, Illinois
Died: February 11, 1876, Heber City, Utah
Husband: Richard Sessions, Private, Company A
Son and Daughter-in-Law: John Sessions and Mary Caroline or Em-
meline Sessions, Private, Company A and Laundress, Company A
Son: William Bradford Sessions, Private, Company A

Elizabeth Garley Shipley
Born: March 25, 1814, Ollaberry, England
Married: 1841, Burton, England
Died: 1846, Mount Pisgah, Iowa
Husband: Joseph Shipley, Private, Company C

Mary Elizabeth Creager Shupe
Born: January 2, 1820, Reed Creek, Virginia
Married: October 12, 1837, Wythe County, Virginia
Died: March 20, 1900, Ogden, Utah
Husband: Andrew Jackson Shupe, Private, Company C

Louisa Maria Rose Sprague
Born: November 24, 1811, Lysle, New York
Married: September 20, 1832, Genesee County, New York
Died: August 5, 1897, Huntsville, Utah
Husband: Richard Demont Sprague, Musician, Company C

Sophronia Arminia Scott Standage
Born: June 13, 1821, Perry, New York
Married: April 13, 1845, Nauvoo, Illinois
Died: July 1, 1896, Mesa, Arizona
Husband: Henry Standage, Private, Company E

Lois Coon Stevens
Born: March 10, 1811, South Crosby, Upper Canada
Married: November 5, 1828, Brockville, Canada
Died: May 30, 1897, Fairview, Utah
Husband: Arnold Stevens, Corporal, Company D

Fanny Parks Taggart
Born: October 25, 1821, Livonia, New York
Married: July 12, 1845, Nauvoo, Illinois
Died: May 6, 1891, Richville, Utah
Husband: George Washington Taggart, Musician, Company B

Abigail Haws Tuttle
Born: June 15, 1828, Upper Canada
Married: July 18, 1846, Council Bluffs, Iowa
Died: September 18, 1849, Iowa
Husband: Luther Terry Tuttle, Sergeant, Company D

Minerva Wade
Born: September 1829, Farmingdale, *State unknown*
Married: May 1, 1849, William Hickman
Died: *Unknown*
Father: Moses Wade, Private, Company C
Brother: Edward Davis Wade, Private, Company C

Sally Maria Bundy Wade
Born: May 13, 1798, Orsego County, New York
Married: 1817, Farmingdale, New York
Died: October 13, 1848, Council Bluffs, Iowa
Husband: Moses Wade, Private, Company C
Son: Edward Davis Wade, Private, Company C

Mary Burrell Woolsey
Born: April 11, 1813, Cincinnati, Ohio
Married: April 25, 1829, Jackson County, Indiana
Died: 1858, Provo, Utah
Husband: Thomas Woolsey, Private, Company E

Margaret Jane Willis Willis
Born: August 17, 1812, Gallatin County, Illinois
Married: March 29, 1833, Illinois
Died: August 13, 1850, buried Salt Lake County, Utah
Husband: William Wesley Willis, 1st Sergeant and 3rd Lieutenant, Company A

Sources Cited

Alexander, Horace Martin. Http://www.cc.utah.edu/~jsg16/HMAlex. htm.

Beaman, Helen Keith. *Edges Disappear.* Salt Lake City: Book Printers of Utah, Inc., 2008.

Bednar, David A. "The Tender Mercies of the Lord," *Ensign,* May, 2005.

Bigler, David L. and Will Bagley, eds. *Army of Israel Mormon Battalion Narratives.* Logan: Utah State University Press, 2000.

Brayman, Mason. *The Evacuation of Nauvoo.* Chapter 20. Http:// www.globusz.com/ebooks/Mormons/00000059.htm

Canfield dates. Http://winterquarters.byu.edu/pages/ward15/pafg15. htm.

Christian hymn, "Sacrifice." Http://www.hymns.me.uk/come-holy-ghost-creator-come.htm.

Cleavinger, Gladys LaVeryl Hall. *My Favorite Wind.* In author's possession.

Extermination Order. Http://en.wikipedia.org/wiki/Extermination_ Order_(Mormonism)#Text_of_the_Order.

Girl I've Left Behind. Http://www.mormonbattalion.com/girl_ive_ left_behind_me.html

Holland, Jeffery R. "The Ministry of Angels," *Ensign,* Nov. 2008.

Howe, Henry. *Historical Collections of the Great West,* vol 2. Cincinnati: E. Morgan and Co., 1851.

Hymns UK. Http://www.hymns.me.uk/come-holy-ghost-creator-come.htm.

Kelly, Brian and Petra. *Latter-day History of the Church of Jesus Christ of Latter-day Saints.* American Fork, Utah: Covenant Communications, 2000.

Laverty, Dane. *Doula Sun.* In author's possession.

Linn, William Alexander. *The Story of the Mormons from the Dates of Their Origin to the Year 1901.* New York: Globusz Publishing, 1901.

Martin Handcart Company. Http://en.wikipedia.org/wiki/Martin_Handcart_Company#1856:_Willie_and_Martin_handcart_companies.

Maynes, Shirley N. *Five Hundred Wagons Stood Still.* Corporate Edge Printing, 1999.

Original Mormon Battalion Song. Http://www.mormonbattalion.com/girl_ive_left_behind_me.html.

Personal History of Mary Lee Bland Ewell. Provided by Kathleen Sheffield. In author's possession.

Personal History of Sarah Beriah Fiske Allen Ricks. Provided by Vera Sears. In author's possession.

Pratt, Parley P. *Autobiography of Parley Pratt,* 3rd ed. Salt Lake City: Deseret Book Company, 1938.

Raymond Family. Http://freepages.genealogy.rootsweb.ancestry.com/~raymondfamily/ddorrisTOC.html.

Ricketts, Norma Baldwin. *The Mormon Battalion: US Army of the West.* Logan: Utah State University Press, 1996.

Smith, Joseph. *History of the Church,* vol. 3. Salt Lake City: Deseret Book Company, 1978.

Taggart, Fanny Parks. Http://www.taggartfamily.org/Wives.htm.

Taggart, George Washington. Http://www.taggartfamily.org/GWT%20by%20Eileen%20Robinson.htm.

Taggart Family Organization. Http://www.taggartfamily.org/GWT%20by%20Eileen%20Robinson.htm,10.

Tyler, Daniel. *A Concise History of the Mormon Battalion in the Mexican War.* Glorieta, New Mexico: The Rio Grande Press, Inc., 1881, 1980.

Winter Quarters. Http://winterquarters.byu.edu/pages/ward15/pafg15.htm.

About the Author

BORN IN MONTANA, CAROLINE JEAN PROHOSKY grew up under the tutelage of a mother who quoted Shakespeare and who loved painting and literature. But Caroline's greatest passion from earliest childhood was dance. Throughout her childhood her parents arranged for her to study ballet whenever circumstances and family funds permitted.

Caroline began her serious training in contemporary dance at Brigham Young University, where she graduated with a BA in 1972. She graduated from the University of California at Los Angeles with an MA in contemporary dance choreography in 1980.

Caroline taught at Ricks College (now BYU–Idaho) before joining the faculty at BYU in 1986. While teaching at BYU, her choreography was honored four times by the American College Dance Festival Association. She directed BYU's Contemporary Dance Theatre for a period of fourteen years, during which time the company performed nationally and internationally in countries such as Turkey, Israel, the Philippines, Korea, South Africa, Australia, and India.

Most recently, Caroline has devoted her creative energy to combining dance and film. She is a convert to The Church of Jesus Christ of Latter-day Saints and served in the Argentina Cordova Mission.